Our Debt to Greece and Rome

EDITORS
GEORGE DEPUE HADZSITS, PH.D.

DAVID MOORE ROBINSON, PH.D., LL.D.

HORACE
AND HIS INFLUENCE

BY
GRANT SHOWERMAN

COOPER SQUARE PUBLISHERS, INC.
NEW YORK
1963

Published 1963 by Cooper Square Publishers, Inc.
59 Fourth Avenue, New York 3, N.Y.
Library of Congress Catalog Card No. 63-10271

PRINTED IN THE UNITED STATES OF AMERICA
by SENTRY PRESS, NEW YORK, N. Y. 10013

To

HOWARD LESLIE SMITH

LOVER OF LETTERS

SABINE HILLS

On Sabine hills when melt the snows,
Still level-full His river flows;
Each April now His valley fills
With cyclamen and daffodils;
And summers wither with the rose.

Swift-waning moons the cycle close:
Birth, — toil, — mirth, — death; life onward goes
Through harvest heat or winter chills
        On Sabine hills.

Yet One breaks not His long repose,
Nor hither comes when Zephyr blows;
In vain the spring's first swallow trills;
Never again that Presence thrills;
One charm no circling season knows
        On Sabine hills.

GEORGE MEASON WHICHER

EDITORS' PREFACE

THE VOLUME on Horace and His Influence by Doctor Showerman is the second to appear in the Series, known as "Our Debt to Greece and Rome."

Doctor Showerman has told the story of this influence in what seems to us the most effective manner possible, by revealing the spiritual qualities of Horace and the reasons for their appeal to many generations of men. These were the crown of the personality and work of the ancient poet, and admiration of them has through successive ages always been a token of aspiration and of a striving for better things.

The purpose of the volumes in this Series will be to show the influence of virtually all of the great forces of the Greek and Roman civilizations upon subsequent life and thought and the extent to which these are interwoven into the fabric of our own life of to-day. Thereby we shall all know more clearly the nature of our inheritance from the past and shall comprehend more steadily the currents of our own life, their direction and their value. This is, we take it, of considerable importance for life as a whole, whether for correct thinking or for true idealism.

The supremacy of Horace within the limits that he set for himself is no fortuity, and the miracle of his achievement will always remain an inspiration for some. But it is not as a distant ideal for a few, but as a living and vital force for all, that we should approach him; and to assist in this is the aim of our little volume.

The significance of Horace to the twentieth century will gain in clarity from an understanding of his meaning to other days. We shall discover that the eternal verity of his message, whether in ethics or in art, comes to *us* with a very particular challenge, warning and cry.

CONTENTS

CHAPTER   PAGE

    INTRODUCTION: THE DYNAMISM OF
    THE FEW   xiii

I. HORACE INTERPRETED
    The Appeal of Horace   3
   1. Horace the Person   6
   2. Horace the Poet   9
   3. Horace the Interpreter of His Times
      Horace the Duality   23
      i. The Interpreter of Italian
         Landscape   25
      ii. The Interpreter of Italian Living   28
      iii. The Interpreter of Roman
         Religion   31
      iv. The Interpreter of the Popular
         Wisdom   35
      Horace and Hellenism.   38
   4. Horace the Philosopher of Life
      Horace the Spectator and Essayist   39
      i. The Vanity of Human Wishes   44
      ii. The Pleasures of this World .   49
      iii. Life and Morality   54
      iv. Life and Purpose   59
      v. The Sources of Happiness . .   62

[xi]

CONTENTS

CHAPTER   PAGE

II. HORACE THROUGH THE AGES

Introductory 69
1. Horace the Prophet 70
2. Horace and Ancient Rome . . . 75
3. Horace and the Middle Age . . . 87
4. Horace and Modern Times
   The Rebirth of Horace 104
   i. In Italy 106
   ii. In France 114
   iii. In Germany 115
   iv. In Spain 118
   v. In England 121
   vi. In the Schools 126

III. HORACE THE DYNAMIC

The Cultivated Few 127
1. Horace and the Literary Ideal . . 131
2. Horace and Literary Creation
   i. The Translator's Ideal 136
   ii. Creation 143
3. Horace in the Living of Men . . 152

IV. CONCLUSION 168
   NOTES AND BIBLIOGRAPHY 171

INTRODUCTION: THE DYNAMISM
OF THE FEW

TO THOSE who stand in the midst of times and attempt to grasp their meaning, civilization often seems hopelessly complicated. The myriad and mysterious interthreading of motive and action, of cause and effect, presents to the near vision no semblance of a pattern, and the whole web is so confused and meaningless that the mind grows to doubt the presence of design, and becomes skeptical of the necessity, or even the importance, of any single strand.

Yet civilization is on the whole a simple and easily understood phenomenon. This is true most apparently of that part of the human family of which Europe and the Americas form the principal portion, and whose influences have made themselves felt also in remote continents. If to us it is less apparently true of the world outside our western civilization, the reason lies in the fact that we are not in possession of equal facilities for the exercise of judgment.

We are all members one of another, and the body which we form is a consistent and more or less unchanging whole. There are certain elemental facts which underlie human society wherever it has advanced to a stage deserving the name of civilization. There is the intellectual impulse, with the restraining influence of reason upon the relations of men. There is the active desire to be in right relation with the unknown, which we call religion. There is the attempt at the beautification of life, which we call art. There is the institution of property. There is the institution of marriage. There is the demand for the purity of woman. There is the insistence upon certain decencies and certain conformities which constitute what is known as morality. There is the exchange of material conveniences called commerce, with its necessary adjunct, the sanctity of obligation. In a word, there are the universal and eternal verities.

Farther, if what we may call the constitution of civilization is thus definite, its physical limits are even more clearly defined. Civilization is a matter of centers. The world is not large, and its government rests upon the shoulders of the few. The metropolis is the index of capacity for good and ill in a national civilization. Its culture is representative of the common life of town and country.

It follows that the history of civilization is a history of the famous gathering-places of men. The story of human progress in the West is the story of Memphis, Thebes, Babylon, Nineveh, Cnossus, Athens, Alexandria, Rome, and of medieval, Renaissance, and modern capitals. History is a stream, in the remoter antiquity of Egypt and Mesopotamia confined within narrow and comparatively definite banks, gathering in volume and swiftness as it flows through Hellenic lands, and at last expanding into the broad and deep basin of Rome, whence its current, dividing, leads away in various channels to other ample basins, perhaps in the course of time to reunite at some great meeting of waters in the New World. To one afloat in the swirl of contradictory eddies, it may be difficult to judge of the whence and whither of the troubled current, but the ascent of the stream and the exploration of the sources of literature and the arts, of morals, politics, and religion, of commerce and mechanics, is on the whole no difficult adventure.

Finally, civilization is not only a matter of local habitation, but a matter of individual men. The great city is both determined by, and determines, its environment; the great man is the product, and in turn the producer, of the culture of his nation. The human race is gregarious and sequacious, rather than individual and adventurous. Progress depends upon the initiative of spirited and gifted men, rather than upon the tardy movement of the mass, upon idea rather than force, upon spirit rather than matter.

I preface my essay with these reflections because there may be readers at first thought skeptical of even modest statements regarding Horace as a force in the history of our culture and a contributor to our life today. It is only when the continuity of history and the essential simplicity and constancy of civilization are understood that the direct and vital connection between past and present is seen, and the mind is no longer startled and incredulous when the historian records that the Acropolis has had more to do with the career of architecture than any other group of buildings in the world, or that the most potent influence in the history of prose is the Latin of Cicero, or that poetic

expression is more choice and many men ap-
preciably saner and happier because of a
Roman poet dead now one thousand nine
hundred and thirty years.

HORACE AND HIS INFLUENCE

HORACE AND HIS
INFLUENCE

I. HORACE INTERPRETED

The Appeal of Horace

IN ESTIMATING the effect of Horace
upon his own and later times, we must take
into account two aspects of his work.
These are, the forms in which he expressed
himself, and the substance of which they are
the garment. We shall find him distinguished
in both; but in the substance of his message
we shall find him distinguished by a quality
which sets him apart from other poets ancient
and modern.

This distinctive quality lies neither in the
originality nor in the novelty of the Horatian
message, which, as a matter of fact, is surpris-
ingly familiar, and perhaps even commonplace.
It lies rather in the appealing manner and mood
of its communication. It is a message living
and vibrant.

[3]

The reason for this is that in Horace we have, above all, a person. No poet speaks from the page with greater directness, no poet establishes so easily and so completely the personal relation with the reader, no poet is remembered so much as if he were a friend in the flesh. In this respect, Horace among poets is a parallel to Thackeray in the field of the novel. What the letters of Cicero are to the intrigue and turmoil of politics, war, and the minor joys and sorrows of private and social life in the last days of the Republic, the lyrics and " Conversations " of Horace are to the mood of the philosophic mind of the early Empire. Both are lights which afford us a clear view of interiors otherwise but faintly illuminated. They are priceless interpreters of their times. In modern times, we make environment interpret the poet. We understand a Tennyson, a Milton, or even a Shakespeare, from our knowledge of the world in which he lived. In the case of antiquity, the process is reversed. We reconstruct the times of Caesar and Augustus from fortunate acquaintance with two of the most representative men who ever possessed the gift of literary genius.

It is because Horace's appeal depends so

largely upon his qualities as a person that our interpretation of him must center about his personal traits. We shall re-present to the imagination his personal appearance. We shall account for the personal qualities which contributed to the poetic gift that set him apart as the interpreter of the age to his own and succeeding generations. We shall observe the natural sympathy with men and things by reason of which he reflects with peculiar faithfulness the life of city and country. We shall become acquainted with the thoughts and the moods of a mind and heart that were nicely sensitive to sight and sound and personal contact. We shall hear what the poet has to say of himself not only as a member of the human family, but as the user of the pen.

This interpretation of Horace as person and poet will be best attempted from his own work, and best expressed in his own phrase. The pages which follow are a manner of Horatian mosaic. They contain little not said or suggested by the poet himself.

1. HORACE THE PERSON

HORACE was of slight stature among even a slight-statured race. At the period when we like him best, when he was growing mellower and better with advancing years, his black hair was more than evenly mingled with grey. The naturally dark and probably not too finely-textured skin of face and expansive forehead was deepened by the friendly breezes of both city and country to the vigorous golden brown of the Italian. Feature and eye held the mirror up to a spirit quick to anger but plenteous in good-nature. Altogether, Horace was a short, rotund man, smiling but serious, of nothing very remarkable either in appearance or in manner, and with a look of the plain citizen. Of all the ancients who have left no material likeness, he is the least difficult to know in person.

We see him in a carriage or at the shows with Maecenas, the Emperor's fastidious counsellor. We have charming glimpses of him enjoying in company the hospitable shade of huge pine and white poplar on the grassy terrace of some rose-perfumed Italian garden with noisy fountain and hurrying stream. He loiters, with eyes

bent on the pavement, along the winding
Sacred Way that leads to the Forum, or on his
way home struggles against the crowd as it
pushes its way down town amid the dust and
din of the busy city. He shrugs his shoulders
in good-humored despair as the sirocco brings
lassitude and irritation from beyond the Medi-
terranean, or he sits huddled up in some village
by the sea, shivering with the winds from the
Alps, reading, and waiting for the first swallow
to herald the spring.

We see him at a mild game of tennis in the
broad grounds of the Campus Martius. We
see him of an evening vagabonding among the
nameless common folk of Rome, engaging in
small talk with dealers in small merchandise.
He may look in upon a party of carousing
friends, with banter that is not without reproof.
We find him lionized in the homes of the first
men of the city in peace and war, where he
mystifies the not too intellectual fair guests with
graceful and provokingly passionless gallantry.
He sits at ease with greater enjoyment under
the opaque vine and trellis of his own garden.
He appears in the midst of his household as it
bustles with preparation for the birthday feast
of a friend, or he welcomes at a less formal

board and with more unrestrained joy the beloved comrade-in-arms of Philippi, prolonging
the genial intercourse

> "*Till Phoebus the red East unbars*
> *And puts to rout the trembling stars.*"

Or we see him bestride an indifferent nag,
cantering down the Appian Way, with its
border of tombs, toward the towering dark-
green summits of the Alban Mount, twenty
miles away, or climbing the winding white road
to Tivoli where it reclines on the nearest slope
of the Sabines, and pursuing the way beyond it
along the banks of headlong Anio where it
rushes from the mountains to join the Tiber.
We see him finally arrived at his Sabine farm,
the gift of Maecenas, standing in tunic-sleeves
at his doorway in the morning sun, and contemplating with thankful heart valley and hillside opposite, and the cold stream of Digentia
in the valley-bottom below. We see him ram-
bling about the wooded uplands of his little
estate, and resting in the shade of a decaying
rustic temple to indite a letter to the friend
whose not being present is all that keeps him
from perfect happiness. He participates with
the near-by villagers in the joys of the rural

[8]

holiday. He mingles homely philosophy and fiction with country neighbors before his own hearth in the big living-room of the farm-house.

Horace's place is not among the dim and uncertain figures of a hoary antiquity. Only give him modern shoes, an Italian cloak, and a walking-stick, instead of sandals and toga, and he may be seen on the streets of Rome today. Nor is he less modern in character and bearing than in appearance. We discern in his composition the same strange and seemingly contradictory blend of the grave and gay, the lively and severe, the constant and the mercurial, the austere and the trivial, the dignified and the careless, that is so baffling to the observer of Italian character and conduct today.

2. HORACE THE POET

To understand how Horace came to be a great poet as well as an engaging person, it is necessary to look beneath this somewhat commonplace exterior, and to discern the spiritual man.

The foundations of literature are laid in life. For the production of great poetry two conditions are necessary. There must be, first, an age pregnant with the celestial fires of deep emotion. Second, there must be in its midst one of the rare men whom we call inspired. He must be of such sensitive spiritual fiber as to vibrate to every breeze of the national passion, of such spiritual capacity as to assimilate the common thoughts and moods of the time, of such fine perception and of such sureness of command over word, phrase, and rhythm, as to give crowning expression to what his soul has made its own.

For abundance of stirring and fertilizing experience, history presents few equals of the times when Horace lived. His lifetime fell in an age which was in continual travail with great and uncertain movement. Never has Fortune taken greater delight in her bitter and insolent game, never displayed a greater pertinacity in the derision of men. In the period from Horace's birth at Venusia in southeastern Italy, on December 8, B.C. 65, to November 27, B.C. 8, when

> " Mourned of men and Muses nine,
>   They laid him on the Esquiline,"

there occurred the series of great events, to men in their midst incomprehensible, bewildering, and disheartening, which after times could readily interpret as the inevitable change from the ancient and decaying Republic to the better knit if less free life of the Empire.

We are at an immense distance, and the differences have long since been composed. The menacing murmur of trumpets is no longer audible, and the seas are no longer red with blood. The picture is old, and faded, and darkened, and leaves us cold, until we illuminate it with the light of imagination. Then first we see, or rather feel, the magnitude of the time: its hatreds and its selfishness; its differences of opinion, sometimes honest and sometimes disingenuous, but always maintained with the heat of passion; its divisions of friends and families; its lawlessness and violence; its terrifying uncertainties and adventurous plunges; its tragedies of confiscation, murder, fire, proscription, feud, insurrection, riot, war; the dramatic exits of the leading actors in the great play, — of Catiline at Pistoria, of Crassus in the eastern deserts, of Clodius at Bovillae within sight of the gates of Rome, of Pompey in Egypt, of Cato in Africa, of Caesar, Servius Sulpicius, Marcellus, Trebonius and Dolabella, Hirtius and Pansa, Decimus Brutus, the Ciceros,

Marcus Brutus and Cassius, Sextus the son of Pompey, Antony and Cleopatra,— as one after another

> "Strutted and fretted his hour upon the stage,
>   And then was heard no more."

It is in relief against a background such as this that Horace's works should be read,— the *Satires*, published in 35 and 30, which the poet himself calls *Sermones*, " Conversations," " Talks," or *Causeries;* the collection of lyrics called *Epodes*, in 29; three books of *Odes* in 23; a book of *Epistles*, or further *Causeries*, in 20; the *Secular Hymn* in 17; a second book of *Epistles* in 14; a fourth book of *Odes* in 13; and a final *Epistle, On the Art of Poetry*, at a later and uncertain date.

It is above all against such a background that Horace's invocation to Fortune should be read:

> *Goddess, at lovely Antium is thy shrine:*
> *Ready art thou to raise with grace divine*
> *Our mortal frame from lowliest dust of earth,*
> *Or turn triumph to funeral for thy mirth;*

or that other expression of the inscrutable uncertainty of the human lot:

[12]

Fortune, whose joy is e'er our woe and shame,
With hard persistence plays her mocking game;
Bestowing favors all inconstantly,
Kindly to others now, and now to me.
With me, I praise her; if her wings she lift
To leave me, I resign her every gift,
And, cloaked about in my own virtue's pride,
Wed honest poverty, the dowerless bride.

Horace is not here the idle singer of an empty day. His utterance may be a universal, but in the light of history it is no commonplace. It is the eloquent record of the life of Rome in an age which for intensity is unparalleled in the annals of the ancient world.

And yet men may live a longer span of years than fell to the lot of Horace, and in times no less pregnant with event, and still fail to come into really close contact with life. Horace's experience was comprehensive, and touched the life of his generation at many points. He was born in a little country town in a province distant from the capital. His father, at one time a slave, and always of humble calling, was a man of independent spirit, robust sense, and excellent character, whose constant and intimate companionship left everlasting gratitude in the heart of the son. He provided for the little Horace's education at first among the sons of the " great " centurions who constituted the society of the garrison-town of Venusia, afterwards ambitiously took him to Rome to acquire even the accomplishments usual among the sons of senators, and finally sent him to Athens, garner of wisdom of the ages, where the learning of the past was constantly made to live again by masters with the quick Athenian spirit of telling or hearing new things.

The intellectual experience of Horace's younger days was thus of the broadest character. Into it there entered and were blended the shrewd practical understanding of the Italian provincial; the ornamental accomplishments of the upper classes; the inspiration of Rome's history, with the long line of heroic figures that. appear in the twelfth *Ode* of the first book like a gallery of magnificent portraits; first-hand knowledge of prominent men of action and letters; unceasing discussion of questions of the day which could be avoided by none; and, finally, humanizing contact on their own soil with Greek philosophy and poetry, Greek monuments and history, and teachers of racial as well as intellectual descent from the greatest people of the past.

But Horace's experience assumed still greater proportions. He passed from the university of Athens to the larger university of life. The news of Caesar's death at the hands of the " Liberators," which reached him as a student there at the age of twenty-one, and the arrival of Brutus some months after, stirred his young blood. As an officer in the army of Brutus, he underwent the hardships of the long campaign, enriching life with new friendships formed in circumstances that have always tightened the friendly bond. He saw the disastrous day of Philippi, narrowly escaped death by shipwreck, and on his return to Italy and Rome found himself without father or fortune.

Nor was the return to Rome the end of his education. In the interval which followed, Horace's mind, always of philosophic bent, was no doubt busy with reflection upon the disparity between the ideals of the liberators and the practical results of their actions, upon the difference between the disorganized, anarchical Rome of the civil war and the gradually knitting Rome of Augustus, and upon the futility of presuming to judge the righteousness either of motives or means in a world where men, to say nothing of understanding each other, could not understand themselves. In the end, he accepted what was not to be avoided. He went farther than acquiescence. The growing conviction among thoughtful men that Augustus was the hope of Rome found lodgment also in his mind. He gravitated from negative to positive. His value as an educated man was recognized, and he found himself at twenty-four in possession of the always coveted boon of the young Italian, a place in the government employ. A clerkship in the treasury gave him salary, safety, respectability, a considerable dignity, and a degree of leisure.

Of the leisure he made wise use. Still in the afterglow of his Athenian experience, he began to write. He attracted the attention of a limited circle of associates. The personal qualities which made him a favorite with the leaders of the Republican army again served him well. He won the recognition and the favor of men who had the ear of the ruling few. In about 33, when he was thirty-two years old, Maecenas, the appreciative counsellor, prompted by Augustus, the politic ruler, who recognized the value of talent in every field for his plans of reconstruction, made him independ-

ent of money-getting, and gave him currency
among the foremost literary men of the city.
He triumphed over the social prejudice against
the son of a freedman, disarmed the jealousy
of literary rivals, and was assured of fame
as well as favor.

Nor was even this the end of Horace's experience with the world of action. It may be
that his actual participation in affairs did cease
with Maecenas's gift of the Sabine farm, and it
is true that he never pretended to live on their
own ground the life of the high-born and rich,
but he nevertheless associated on sympathetic
terms with men through whom he felt all the
activities and ideals of the class most representative of the national life, and past experiences and natural adaptability enabled him to
assimilate their thoughts and emotions.

Thanks to the glowing personal nature of
Horace's works, we know who many of these
friends and patrons were who so enlarged his
vision and deepened his inspiration. Almost
without exception his poems are addressed or
dedicated to men with whom he was on terms of
more than ordinary friendship. They were
rare men, — fit audience, though few; men of
experience in affairs at home and in the field,

men of natural taste and real cultivation, of
broad and sane outlook, of warm heart and
deep sympathies. There was Virgil, whom he
calls the half of his own being. There was
Plotius, and there was Varius, bird of Maeonian
song, whom he ranks with the singer of the
Aeneid himself as the most luminously pure of
souls on earth. There was Quintilius, whose
death was bewailed by many good men; —
when would incorruptible Faith and Truth find
his equal? There was Maecenas, well-bred and
worldly-wise, the pillar and ornament of his
fortunes. There was Septimius, the hoped-for
companion of his mellow old age in the little
corner of earth that smiled on him beyond all
others. There was Iccius, procurator of Agrippa's estates in Sicily, sharing Horace's delight
in philosophy. There was Agrippa himself, son-
in-law of Augustus, grave hero of battles and
diplomacy. There was elderly Trebatius, sometime friend of Cicero and Caesar, with dry
legal humor early seasoned in the wilds of
Gaul. There were Pompeius and Corvinus,
old-soldier friends with whom he exchanged
reminiscences of the hard campaign. There
was Messalla, a fellow-student at Athens, and
Pollio, soldier, orator, and poet. There were

[18]

Julius Florus and other members of the ambitious literary cohort in the train of Tiberius. There was Aristius Fuscus, the watch of whose wit was ever wound and ready to strike. There was Augustus himself, busy administrator of a world, who still found time for letters.

It is through the medium of personalities like these that Horace's message was delivered to the world of his time and to later generations. How far the finished elegance of his expression is due to their discriminating taste, and how much of the breadth and sanity of his content is due to their vigor of character and cosmopolitan culture, we may only conjecture. Literature is not the product of a single individual. The responsive and stimulating audience is hardly less needful than the poet's inspiration.

Such were the variety and abundance of Horace's experience. It was large and human. He had touched life high and low, bond and free, public and private, military and civil, provincial and urban, Hellenic, Asiatic, and Italian, urban and rustic, ideal and practical, at the cultured court and among the ignorant, but not always unwise, common people.

And yet, numbers of men possessed of experience as abundant have died without being poets, or even wise men. Their experience was held in solution, so to speak, and failed to precipitate. Horace's experience did precipitate. Nature gave him the warm and responsive soul by reason of which he became a part of all he met. Unlike most of his associates among the upper classes to which he rose, his sympathies could include the freedman, the peasant, and the common soldier. Unlike most of the multitude from which he sprang, he could extend his sympathies to the careworn rich and the troubled statesman. He had learned from his own lot and from observation that no life was wholly happy, that the cares of the so-called fortunate were only different from, not less real than, those of the ordinary man, that every human heart had its chamber furnished for the entertainment of Black Care, and that the chamber was never without its guest.

But not even the precipitate of experience called wisdom will alone make the poet. Horace was again endowed by nature with another and rarer and equally necessary gift, — the sense of artistic expression. It would be waste of time to debate how much he owed to native genius, how much to his own laborious patience, and how much to the good fortune of generous human contact. He is surely to be classed among examples of what for want of a better term we call inspiration. The poet *is* born. We may account for the inspiration of Horace by supposing him of Greek descent (as if Italy had never begotten poets of her own), but the mystery remains. In the case of any poet, after everything has been said of the usual influences, there is always something left to be accounted for only on the ground of genius. It was the possession of this that set Horace apart from other men of similar experience.

The poet, however, is not the mere accident of birth. Horace is aware of a power not himself that makes for poetic righteousness, and realizes the mystery of inspiration. The Muse cast upon him at birth her placid glance. He expects glory neither on the field nor in the course, but looks to song for his triumphs. To Apollo,

> "*Lord of the enchanting shell,*
>   *Parent of sweet and solemn-breathing airs,*"

who can give power of song even unto the mute, he owes all his power and all his fame. It is the gift of Heaven that he is pointed out by the finger of the passer-by as the minstrel of the Roman lyre, that he breathes the divine fire and pleases men. But he is as perfectly appreciative of the fact that poets are born and also made, and condemns the folly of depending upon inspiration unsupported by effort. He calls himself the bee of Matinum, industriously flitting with honeyed thigh about the banks of humid Tibur. What nature begins, cultivation must develop. Neither training without the rich vein of native endowment, nor natural talent without cultivation, will suffice; both must be friendly conspirators in the process of forming the poet. Wisdom is the beginning and source of writing well. He who would run with success the race that is set before him must endure from boyhood the hardships of heat and cold, and abstain from women and wine. The gift of God must be made perfect by the use of the file, by long waiting, and by conscious intellectual discipline.

3. HORACE THE INTERPRETER OF HIS TIMES

HORACE THE DUALITY

VARIED as were Horace's experiences, they were mainly of two kinds, and there are two Horaces who reflect them. There is a more natural Horace, simple and direct, of ordinary Italian manners and ideals, and a less natural Horace, finished in the culture of Greece and the artificialities of life in the capital. They might be called the unconventional and the conventional Horace.

This duality is only the reflection of the two-fold experience of Horace as the provincial village boy and as the successful literary man of the city. The impressions received from Venusia and its simple population of hard-working, plain-speaking folk, from the roaring Aufidus and the landscape of Apulia, from the freedman father's common-sense instruction as he walked about in affectionate companionship with his son, never faded from Horace's mind. The ways of the city were superimposed upon the ways of the country, but never displaced nor even covered them. They were a garment put on and off, sometimes partly hiding, but never for long, the original cloak of simplicity. It is not necessary to think its wearer insincere when, constrained by social circumstance, he put it on. As in most dualities not consciously assumed, both Horaces were genuine. When Davus the slave reproaches his master for longing, while at Rome, to be back in the country, and for praising the attractions of the city, while in the country, it is not mere discontent or inconsistency in Horace which he is attacking. Horace loved both city and country.

And yet, whatever the appeal of the city and its artificialities, Horace's real nature called for the country and its simple ways. It is the Horace of Venusia and the Sabines who is the more genuine of the two. The more formal poems addressed to Augustus and his household sometimes sound the note of affectation, but the most exacting critic will hesitate to bring a like charge against the odes which celebrate the fields and hamlets of Italy and the prowess of her citizen-soldiers of time gone by, or against the mellow epistles and lyrics in which the poet philosophizes upon the spectacle of human life.

i. THE INTERPRETER OF ITALIAN
LANDSCAPE

The real Horace is to be found first of all as
the interpreter of the beauty and fruitfulness
of Italy. It is no land of mere literary imagination which he makes us see with such clear-cut
distinctness. It is not an Italy in Theocritean
colors, like the Italy of Virgil's *Bucolics,* but
the Italy of Horace's own time, the Italy of
his own birth and experience, and the Italy of
today. Horace is not a descriptive poet. The
reader will look in vain for nature-poems in
the modern sense. With a word or a phrase
only, he flashes upon our vision the beautiful,
the significant, the permanent in the scenery of
Italy. The features which he loved best, or
which for other reasons caught his eye, are
those that we still see. There are the oak and
the opaque ilex, the pine and the poplar, the
dark, funereal cypress, the bright flower of the
too-short-lived rose, and the sweet-scented bed
of violets. There are the olive groves of Venafrum. Most lovely of sights and most beautiful of figures, there is the purple-clustered vine
of vari-colored autumn wedded to the elm.
There is the bachelor plane-tree. There are

the long-horned, grey-flanked, dark-muzzled, liquid-eyed cattle, grazing under the peaceful skies of the Campagna or enjoying in the meadow their holiday freedom from the plow; the same cattle that Carducci sings —

" In the grave sweetness of whose tranquil eyes
Of emerald, broad and still reflected, dwells
All the divine green silence of the plain."

We are made to see the sterile rust on the corn, and to feel the blazing heat of dog-days, when not a breath stirs as the languid shepherd leads his flock to the banks of the stream. The sunny pastures of Calabria lie spread before us, we see the yellow Tiber at flood, the rushing Anio, the deep eddyings of Liris' taciturn stream, the secluded valleys of the Apennines, the leaves flying before the wind at the coming of winter, the snow-covered uplands of the Alban hills, the mead sparkling with hoar-frost at the approach of spring, autumn rearing from the fields her head decorous with mellow fruits, and golden abundance pouring forth from a full horn her treasures upon the land. It is real Italy which Horace cuts on his cameos, — real landscape, real flowers and fruits, real men.

[26]

" What joy there is in these songs! "

writes Andrew Lang, in *Letters to Dead Authors,* " what delight of life, what an exquisite Hellenic grace of art, what a manly nature to endure, what tenderness and constancy of friendship, what a sense of all that is fair in the glittering stream, the music of the waterfall, the hum of bees, the silvery gray of the olive woods on the hillside! How human are all your verses, Horace! What a pleasure is yours in the straining poplars, swaying in the wind! What gladness you gain from the white crest of Soracte, beheld through the fluttering snowflakes while the logs are being piled higher on the hearth! . . . None of the Latin poets your fellows, or none but Virgil, seem to me to have known as well as you, Horace, how happy and fortunate a thing it was to be born in Italy. You do not say so, like your Virgil, in one splendid passage, numbering the glories of the land as a lover might count the perfections of his mistress. But the sentiment is ever in your heart, and often on your lips. ' Me neither resolute Sparta nor the rich Larissaean plain so enraptures as the fane of echoing Albunea, the headlong Anio, the grove of Tibur, the orchards watered by the wandering rills.' So a poet should speak, and to every singer his own land should be dearest. Beautiful is Italy, with the grave and delicate outlines of her sacred hills, her dark groves, her little cities perched like eyries on the crags, her rivers gliding under ancient walls: beautiful is Italy, her seas and her suns."

ii. THE INTERPRETER OF ITALIAN LIVING

Again, in its visualization of the life of Italy, Horace's art is no less clear than in the presentation of her scenery. Where else may be seen so many vivid incidental pictures of men at their daily occupations of work or play? In *Satire* and *Epistle* this is to be expected, though there are satirists and writers of letters who never transfer the colors of life to their canvas; but the lyrics, too, are kaleidoscopic with scenes from the daily round of human life. We are given fleeting but vivid glimpses into the career of merchant and sailor. We see the sportsman in chase of the boar, the rustic setting snares for the greedy thrush, the serenader under the casement, the plowman at his ingleside, the anxious mother at the window on

the cliff, never taking her eyes from the curved
shore, the husbandman passing industrious days
on his own hillside, tilling his own acres with
his own oxen, and training the vine to the un-
wedded tree, the young men of the hill-towns
carrying bundles of fagots along rocky slopes,
the rural holiday and its festivities, the sun-
browned wife making ready the evening meal
against the coming of the tired peasant. We
are shown all the quaint and quiet life of the
countryside.

The page is often golden with homely precept or tale of the sort which for all time has
been natural to farmer folk. There is the story
of the country mouse and the town mouse, the
fox and the greedy weasel that ate until he
could not pass through the crack by which he
came, the rustic who sat and waited for the
river to get by, the horse that called man to aid
him against the stag, and received the bit forever. The most formal and dignified of the
Odes are not without the mellow charm of
Italian landscape and the genial warmth of
Italian life. Even in the first six *Odes* of the
third book, often called the *Inaugural Odes,*
we get such glimpses as the vineyard and the
hailstorm, the Campus Martius on election day,

the soldier knowing no fear, cheerful amid
hardships under the open sky, the restless
Adriatic, the Bantine headlands and the low-
lying Forentum of the poet's infancy, the babe
in the wood of Voltur, the Latin hill-towns, the
craven soldier of Crassus, and the stern patriotism of Regulus. Without these the *In-
augurals* would be but barren and cold, to say
nothing of the splendid outburst against the
domestic degradation of the time, so full of
color and heat and picturesqueness:

'Twas not the sons of parents such as these
That tinged with Punic blood the rolling seas,
Laid low the cruel Hannibal, and brought
Great Pyrrhus and Antiochus to naught;

But the manly brood of rustic soldier folk,
Taught, when the mother or the father spoke
The word austere, obediently to wield
The heavy mattock in the Sabine field,

Or cut and bear home fagots from the height,
As mountain shadows deepened into night,
And the sun's car, departing down the west,
Brought to the wearied steer the friendly rest.

iii. THE INTERPRETER OF ROMAN RELIGION

Still farther, Horace is an eloquent interpreter of the religion of the countryside. He knows, of course, the gods of Greece and the East,— Venus of Cythera and Paphos, of Eryx and Cnidus, Mercury, deity of gain and benefactor of men, Diana, Lady of the mountain and the glade, Delian Apollo, who bathes his unbound locks in the pure waters of Castalia, and Juno, sister and consort of fulminating Jove. He is impressed by the glittering pomp of religious processions winding their way to the summit of the Capitol. In all this, and even in the emperor-worship, now in its first stages at Rome and more political than religious, he acquiesces, though he may himself be a sparing frequenter of the abodes of worship. For him, as for Cicero, religion is one of the social and civic proprieties, a necessary part of the national mechanism.

But the great Olympic deities do not really stir Horace's enthusiasm, or even evoke his warm sympathy. The only *Ode* in which he prays to one of them with really fervent heart stands alone among all the odes to the national gods. He petitions the great deity of healing

and poetry for what we know is most precious
to him:

"When, kneeling at Apollo's shrine,
   The bard from silver goblet pours
Libations due of votive wine,
   What seeks he, what implores?

"Not harvests from Sardinia's shore;
   Not grateful herds that crop the lea
In hot Calabria; not a store
   Of gold, and ivory;

"Not those fair lands where slow and deep
   Thro' meadows rich and pastures gay
Thy silent waters, Liris, creep,
   Eating the marge away.

"Let him to whom the gods award
   Calenian vineyards prune the vine;
The merchant sell his balms and nard,
   And drain the precious wine

"From cups of gold — to Fortune dear
   Because his laden argosy
Crosses, unshattered, thrice a year
   The storm-vexed Midland sea.

" R*ipe berries from the olive bough,*
  M*allows and endives, be my fare.*
S*on of Latona, hear my vow!*
A*pollo, grant my prayer!*

" H*ealth to enjoy the blessings sent*
  F*rom heaven; a mind unclouded, strong;*
A *cheerful heart; a wise content;*
A*n honored age; and song."*

This is not the prayer of the city-bred formalist. It reflects the heart of humble breed-
ing and sympathies. For the faith which really
sets the poet aglow we must go into the fields
and hamlets of Italy, among the householders
who were the descendants of the long line of
Italian forefathers that had worshiped from
time immemorial the same gods at the same
altars in the same way. They were not the
gods of yesterday, imported from Greece and
Egypt, and splendid with display, but the
simple gods of farm and fold native to the soil
of Italy. Whatever his conception of the
logic of it all, Horace felt a powerful appeal
as he contemplated the picturesqueness of the
worship and the simplicity of the worshiper,
and reflected upon its genuineness and purity
as contrasted with what his worldly wisdom
told him of the heart of the urban worshiper.

Horace may entertain a well-bred skepticism of Jupiter's thunderbolt, and he may pass the jest on the indifference of the Epicurean gods to the affairs of men. When he does so, it is with the gods of mythology and literature he is dealing, not with really religious gods. For the old-fashioned faith of the country he entertains only the kindliest regard. The images that rise in his mind at the mention of religion pure and undefiled are not the gaudy spectacles to be seen in the marbled streets of the capital. They are images of incense rising in autumn from the ancient altar on the homestead, of the feast of the Terminalia with its slain lamb, of libations of ruddy wine and offerings of bright flowers on the clear waters of some ancestral spring, of the simple hearth of the farmhouse, of the family table resplendent with the silver *salinum*, heirloom of generations, from which the grave paterfamilias makes the pious offering of crackling salt and meal to little gods crowned with rosemary and myrtle, of the altar beneath the pine to the Virgin goddess, of Faunus the shepherd-god, in the humor of wooing, roaming the sunny farmfields in quest of retreating wood-nymphs, of Priapus the garden-god, and Silvanus, guardian of boundaries, and, most of all, and typifying all, of the faith of rustic Phidyle, with clean hands and a pure heart raising palms to heaven at the new of the moon, and praying for the full-hanging vine, thrifty fields of corn, and unblemished lambs. Of the religious life represented by these, Horace is no more tempted to make light than he is tempted to delineate the Italian rustic as De Maupassant does the French, — as an amusing animal, with just enough of the human in his composition to make him ludicrous.

iv. THE INTERPRETER OF THE POPULAR WISDOM

Finally, in the homely, unconventional wisdom which fills *Satire* and *Epistle* and sparkles from the *Odes,* Horace is again the national interpreter. The masses of Rome or Italy had little consciously to do with either Stoicism or Epicureanism. Their philosophy was vigorous common sense, and was learned from living, not from conning books. Horace, too, for all his having been a student of formal philosophy in Athens, for all his professed faith in philosophy as a boon for rich and poor and old and young, and for all his inclination to yield to the natural human impulse toward system and adopt the philosophy of one of the Schools, is a consistent follower of neither Stoic nor Epicurean. Both systems attracted him by their virtues, and both repelled him because of their weaknesses. His half-humorous confession of wavering allegiance is only a reflection of the shiftings of a mind open to the appeal of both:

And, lest you inquire under what guide or to what hearth I look for safety, I will tell you that I am sworn to obedience in no master's formula, but am a guest in whatever haven the tempest sweeps me to. Now I am full of action and deep in the waves of civic life, an unswerving follower and guardian of the true virtue, now I secretly backslide to the precepts of Aristippus, and try to bend circumstance to myself, not myself to circumstance.

Horace is either Stoic or Epicurean, or neither, or both. The character of philosophy depends upon definition of terms, and Epicureanism with Horace's definitions of pleasure and duty differed little in practical working from Stoicism. In profession, he was more of the Epicurean; in practice, more of the Stoic. His philosophy occupies ground between both, or, rather, ground common to both. It admits of no name. It is not a system. It owes its resemblances to either of the Schools more to his own nature than to his familiarity with them, great as that was.

The foundations of Horace's philosophy were laid before he ever heard of the Schools. Its basis was a habit of mind acquired by association with his father and the people of Venusia, and with the ordinary people of Rome. Under the influence of reading, study, and social converse at Athens, under the stress of experience in the field, and from long contemplation of life in the large in the capital of an empire, it crystallized into a philosophy of life. The term " philosophy " is misleading in Horace's case. It suggests books and formulae and externals. What Horace read in books did not all remain for him the dead philosophy of ink and paper; what was in tune with his nature he assimilated, to become philosophy in action, philosophy which really was the guide of life. His faith in it is unfeigned:

Thus does the time move slowly and ungraciously which hinders me from the active realization of what, neglected, is a harm to young and old alike. . . . The envious man, the ill-tempered, the indolent, the wine-bibber, the too free lover,— no mortal, in short, is so crude that his nature cannot be made more gentle if only he will lend a willing ear to cultivation.

The occasional phraseology of the Schools which Horace employs should not mislead. It is for the most part the convenient dress for truth discovered for himself through experience; or it may be literary ornament. The humorous and not unsatiric lines to his poet-friend Albius Tibullus,— " when you want a good laugh, come and see me; you will find me fat and sleek and my skin well cared for, a pig from the sty of Epicurus," — are as easily the jest of a Stoic as the confession of an Epicurean. Horace's philosophy is individual and natural, and representative of Roman common sense rather than any School.

HORACE AND HELLENISM

A word should be said here regarding the frequent use of the word " Hellenic " in connection with Horace's genius. Among the results of his higher education, it is natural

[38]

that none should be more prominent to the eye than the influence of Greek letters upon his work; but to call Horace Greek is to be blinded to the essential by the presence in his poems of Greek form and Greek allusion. It would be as little reasonable to call a Roman triumphal arch Greek because it displays column, architrave, or a facing of marble from Greece. What makes Roman architecture stand is not ornament, but Roman concrete and the Roman vault. Horace is Greek as Milton is Hebraic or Roman, or as Shakespeare is Italian.

4. HORACE THE PHILOSOPHER OF LIFE

HORACE THE SPECTATOR AND ESSAYIST

A GREAT source of the richness of personality which constitutes Horace's principal charm is to be found in his contemplative disposition. His attitude toward the universal drama is that of the onlooker. As we shall see, he is not without keen interest in the piece, but his prevailing mood is that of mild amusement. In time past, he has himself assumed more than one of the rôles, and has known personally many of the actors. He

knows perfectly well that there is a great
deal of the mask and buskin on the stage of
life, and that each man in his time plays many
parts. Experience has begotten reflection, and
reflection has contributed in turn to experience,
until contemplation has passed from diversion
to habit.

Horace is another Spectator, except that his
" meddling with any practical part in life " has
not been so slight:

Thus I live in the world rather as a Spectator of mankind than as one of the species,
by which means I have made myself a specu-
lative statesman, soldier, merchant, and arti-
san, without ever meddling with any practical
part in life. I am very well versed in the
theory of a husband, or a father, and can discern the errors in the economy, business, and
diversion of others, better than those who are
engaged in them: as standers-by discover blots
which are apt to escape those who are in the
game.

He looks down from his post upon the life of
men with as clear vision as Lucretius, whom he
admires:

Nothing is sweeter than to dwell in the
lofty citadels secure in the wisdom of the sages,

thence to look down upon the rest of mankind blindly wandering in mistaken paths in the search for the way of life, striving one with another in the contest of wits, emulous in distinction of birth, night and day straining with supreme effort at length to arrive at the heights of power and become lords of the world.

Farther, Horace is not merely the stander-by contemplating the game in which objective mankind is engaged. He is also a spectator of himself. Horace the poet-philosopher contemplates Horace the man with the same quiet amusement with which he surveys the human family of which he is an inseparable yet detachable part. It is the universal aspect of Horace which is the object of his contemplation,— Horace playing a part together with the rest of mankind in the infinitely diverting *comédie humaine*. He uses himself, so to speak, for illustrative purposes, — to point the moral of the genuine; to demonstrate the indispensability of hard work as well as genius; to afford concrete proof of the possibility of happiness without wealth. He is almost as objective to himself as the landscape of the Sabine farm. Horace the spectator sees Horace the man against the background of human life just as he sees snow-mantled Soracte, or the cold Digentia, or the restless Adriatic, or leafy Tarentum, or snowy Algidus, or green Venafrum. The clear-cut elegance of his miniatures of Italian scenery is not due to their individual interest, but to their connection with the universal life of man. Description for its own sake is hardly to be found in Horace. In the same way, the vivid glimpses he affords of his own life, person, and character almost never prompt the thought of egotism. The most personal of poets, his expression of self nowhere becomes selfish expression.

But there are spectators who are mere spectators. Horace is more; he is a critic and an interpreter. He looks forth upon life with a keen vision for comparative values, and gives sane and distinct expression to what he sees.

Horace must not be thought of, however, as a censorious or carping critic. His attitude is judicial, and the verdict is seldom other than lenient and kindly. He is not a wasp of Twickenham, not a Juvenal furiously laying about him with a heavy lash, not a Lucilius with the axes of Scipionic patrons to grind, having at the leaders of the people and the people themselves. He is in as little degree an Ennius, composing merely to gratify the taste for entertainment. There are some, as a matter of fact, to whom in satire he seems to go beyond the limit of good-nature. At vice in pronounced form, at all forms of unmanliness, he does indeed strike out, like Lucilius the knight of Campania, his predecessor and pattern, gracious only to virtue and to the friends of virtue; but those whose hands are clean and whose hearts are pure need fear nothing. Even those who are guilty of the ordinary frailties of human kind need fear nothing worse than being good-humoredly laughed at. The objects of Horace's smiling condemnation are not the trifling faults of the individual or the class, but the universal grosser stupidities which poison the sources of life.

The Horace of the *Satires* and *Epistles* is better called an essayist. That he is a satirist at all is less by virtue of intention than because of the mere fact that he is a spectator. To look upon life with the eye of understanding is to see men the prey to passions and delusions, — the very comment on which can be nothing else than satire.

And now, what is it that Horace sees as he

sits in philosophic detachment on the serene heights of contemplation; and what are his reflections?

The great factor in the character of Horace is his philosophy of life. To define it is to give the meaning of the word Horatian as far as content is concerned, and to trace the thread which more than any other makes his works a unity.

i. THE VANITY OF HUMAN WISHES

Horace looks forth upon a world of discontented and restless humanity. The soldier, the lawyer, the farmer, the trader, swept over the earth in the passion for gain, like dust in the whirlwind, — all are dissatisfied. Choose anyone you will from the midst of the throng; either with greed for money or with miserable ambition for power, his soul is in travail. Some are dazzled by fine silver, some lose their senses over bronze. Some are ever straining after the prizes of public life. There are many who love not wisely, but too well. Most are engaged in a mad race for money, whether to assure themselves of retirement and ease in old age, or out of the sportsman's desire to outstrip their rivals in the course. As many as are mortal men, so many are the objects of their pursuit.

And, over and about all men, by reason of their bondage to avarice, ambition, appetite, and passion, hovers Black Care. It flits above their sleepless eyes in the panelled ceiling of the darkened palace, it sits behind them on the courser as they rush into battle, it dogs them as they are at the pleasures of the bronze-trimmed yacht. It pursues them everywhere, swifter than the deer, swifter than the wind that drives before it the storm-cloud. Not even those who are most happy are entirely so. No lot is wholly blest. Perfect happiness is unattainable. Tithonus, with the gift of ever-lasting life, wasted away in undying old age. Achilles, with every charm of youthful strength and gallantry, was doomed to early death. Not even the richest are content. Something is always lacking in the midst of abundance, and desire more than keeps pace with satisfaction.

Nor are the multitude less enslaved to their desires than the few. Glory drags bound to her glittering chariot-wheels the nameless as well as the nobly-born. The poor are as incon-stant as the rich. What of the man who is not rich? You may well smile. He changes from garret to garret, from bed to bed, from bath to bath and barber to barber, and is just as seasick in a hired boat as the wealthy man on board his private yacht.

And not only are all men the victims of insatiable desire, but all are alike subject to the uncertainties of fate. Insolent Fortune without notice flutters her swift wings and leaves them. Friends prove faithless, once the cask is drained to the lees. Death, unforeseen and unexpected, lurks in ambush for them in a thousand places. Some are swallowed up by the greedy sea. Some the Furies give to destruction in the grim spectacle of war. Without respect of age or person, the ways of death are thronged with young and old. Cruel Proserpina passes no man by.

Even they who for the time escape the object of their dread must at last face the inevitable. Invoked or not invoked, Death comes to release the lowly from toil, and to strip the proud of power. The same night awaits all; everyone must tread once for all the path of death. The summons is delivered impartially at the hovels of the poor and the turreted palaces of the rich. The dark stream must be crossed by prince and peasant alike.

Eternal exile is the lot of all, whether nameless
and poor, or sprung of the line of Inachus:

*Alas! my Postumus, alas! how speed
The passing years: nor can devotion's deed
Stay wrinkled age one moment on its way,
Nor stay one moment death's appointed day;*

*Not though with thrice a hundred oxen slain
Each day thou prayest Pluto to refrain,
The unmoved by tears, who threefold Geryon drave,
And Tityus, beneath the darkening wave.*

*The wave we all must one day surely sail
Who live and breathe within this mortal vale,
Whether our lot with princely rich to fare,
Whether the peasant's lowly life to share.*

*In vain for us from murderous Mars to flee,
In vain to shun the storms of Hadria's sea,
In vain to fear the poison-laden breath
Of Autumn's sultry south-wind, fraught with death;*

*Adown the wandering stream we all must go,
Adown Cocytus' waters, black and slow;
The ill-famed race of Danaus all must see,
And Sisyphus, from labors never free.*

All must be left,— lands, home, beloved wife,—
All left behind when we have done with life;
One tree alone, of all thou holdest dear,
Shall follow thee, — the cypress, o'er thy bier!

Thy wiser heir will soon drain to their lees
The casks now kept beneath a hundred keys;
The proud old Caecuban will stain the floor,
More fit at pontiffs' solemn feasts to pour.

Nor is there a beyond filled with brightness for the victim of fate to look to. Orcus is unpitying. Mercury's flock of souls is of sable hue, and Proserpina's realm is the hue of the dusk. Black Care clings to poor souls even beyond the grave. Dull and persistent, it is the only substantial feature of the insubstantial world of shades. Sappho still sighs there for love of her maiden companions, the plectrum of Alcaeus sounds its chords only to songs of earthly hardships by land and sea, Prometheus and Tantalus find no surcease from the pangs of torture, Sisyphus ever rolls the returning stone, and the Danaids fill the ever-emptying jars.

ii. THE PLEASURES OF THIS WORLD

The picture is dark with shadow, and must be relieved with light and color. The hasty conclusion should not be drawn that this is the philosophy of gloom. The tone of Horace is neither that of the cheerless skeptic nor that of the despairing pessimist. He does not rise from his contemplation with the words or the feeling of Lucretius:

O miserable minds of men, O blind hearts! In what obscurity and in what dangers is passed this uncertain little existence of yours!

He would have agreed with the philosophy of pessimism that life contains striving and pain, but he would not have shared in the gloom of a Schopenhauer, who in all will sees action, in all action want, in all want pain, who looks upon pain as the essential condition of will, and sees no end of suffering except in the surrender of the will to live. The vanity of human wishes is no secret to Horace, but life is not to him " a soap-bubble which we blow out as long and as large as possible, though each of us knows perfectly well it must sooner or later burst."

No, life may have its inevitable pains and

[49]

its inevitable end, but it is far more substantial in composition than a bubble. For those who possess the secret of detecting and enjoying them, it contains solid goods in abundance.

What is the secret?

The first step toward enjoyment of the human lot is acquiescence. Of course existence has its evils and bitter end, but these are minimized for the man who frankly faces them, and recognizes the futility of struggling against the fact. How much better to endure whatever our lot shall impose. Quintilius is dead: it is hard; but patience makes lighter the ill that fate will not suffer us to correct.

And then, when we have once yielded, and have ceased to look upon perfect happiness as a possibility, or upon any measure of happiness as a right to be demanded, we are in position to take the second step; namely, to make wise use of life's advantages:

Mid all thy hopes and all thy cares, mid all thy
wraths and fears,
Think every shining day that dawns the period to
thy years.
The hour that comes unlooked for is the hour that
doubly cheers.

[50]

Because there are many things to make life
a pleasure. There is the solace of literature;
Black Care is lessened by song. There are
the riches of philosophy, there is the diversion of moving among men. There are the
delights of the country and the town. Above
all, there are friends with whom to share the
joy of mere living in Italy. For what purpose,
if not to enjoy, are the rose, the pine, and the
poplar, the gushing fountain, the generous wine
of Formian hill and Massic slope, the villa by
the Tiber, the peaceful and healthful seclusion
of the Sabines, the pleasing change from the
sharp winter to the soft zephyrs of spring,
the apple-bearing autumn, — "season of
mists and mellow fruitfulness" ? What need
to be unhappy in the midst of such a
world?

And the man who is wise will not only recognize the abounding possibilities about him, but
will seize upon them before they vanish. Who
knows whether the gods above will add a tomorrow to the to-day? Be glad, and lay hand upon
the gifts of the passing hour! Take advantage of the day, and have no silly faith in the
morrow. It is as if Omar were translating
Horace:

" *Waste not your Hour, nor in the vain pursuit*
Of This and That endeavor and dispute;
Better be jocund with the fruitful Grape
Than sadden after none, or bitter, Fruit.

" *Ah! fill the Cup: what boots it to repeat*
How Time is slipping underneath our Feet:
Unborn TOMORROW, *and dead* YESTERDAY,
Why fret about them if TODAY *be sweet!* "

The goods of existence must be enjoyed here
and now, or never, for all must be left behind.
What once is enjoyed is forever our very own.
Happy is the man who can say, at each day's
close, " I have lived! " The day is his, and
cannot be recalled. Let Jove overcast with
black cloud the heavens of to-morrow, or let
him make it bright with clear sunshine, —as he
pleases; what the flying hour of to-day has
already given us he never can revoke. Life
is a stream, now gliding peacefully onward in
mid-channel to the Tuscan sea, now tumbling
upon its swirling bosom the wreckage of flood
and storm. The pitiful human being on its
banks, ever looking with greedy expectation
up the stream, or with vain regret at what is
past, is left at last with nothing at all. The
part of wisdom and of happiness is to keep

eyes on that part of the stream directly before
us, the only part which is ever really seen.

You see how, deep with gleaming snow,
Soracte stands, and, bending low,
    Yon branches droop beneath their burden,
        And streams o'erfrozen have ceased their flow.

Away with cold! the hearth pile high
With blazing logs; the goblet ply
    With cheering Sabine, Thaliarchus;
        Draw from the cask of long years gone by.

All else the gods entrust to keep,
Whose nod can lull the winds to sleep,
    Vexing the ash and cypress agèd,
        Or battling over the boiling deep.

Seek not to pierce the morrow's haze,
But for the moment render praise;
    Nor spurn the dance, nor love's sweet passion,
        Ere age draws on with its joyless days.

Now should the campus be your joy,
And whispered loves your lips employ,
    What time the twilight shadows gather,
        And tryst you keep with the maiden coy.

[53]

From near-by nook her laugh makes plain
Where she had meant to hide, in vain!
How arch her struggles o'er the token
From yielding which she can scarce refrain!

iii. LIFE AND MORALITY

But Horace's Epicureanism never goes to the length of Omar's. He would have shrunk from the Persian as extreme:

" YESTERDAY *This Day's Madness did prepare,*
TOMORROW'S *Silence, Triumph, or Despair,*
Drink! for you know not whence you came,
nor why:
Drink! for you know not why you go, nor where."

The Epicureanism of Horace is more nearly that of Epicurus himself, the saintly recluse who taught that " to whom little is not enough, nothing is enough," and who regarded plain living as at the same time a duty and a happiness. The lives of too liberal disciples have been a slander on the name of Epicurus. Horace is not among them. With degenerate Epicureans, whose philosophy permitted them "To roll with pleasure in a sensual sty," he had little in common. The extraction from life of the honey of enjoyment was indeed the highest purpose, but the purpose could never be realized without the exercise of discrimination, moderation, and a measure of spiritual culture. Life was an art, symmetrical, unified, reposeful, — like the poem of perfect art, or the statue, or the temple. In actual conduct, the hedonist of the better type differed little from the Stoic himself.

The gracious touch and quiet humor with which Horace treats even the most serious themes are often misleading. This effect is the more possible by reason of the presence among his works of passages, not many and for the most part youthful, in which he is guilty of too great freedom.

Horace is really a serious person. He is even something of a preacher, a praiser of the time when he was a boy, a censor and corrector of his youngers. So far as popular definitions of Stoic and Epicurean are concerned, he is much more the former than the latter.

For Horace's counsel is always for moderation, and sometimes for austerity. He is not a wine-bibber, and he is not a total abstainer. To be the latter on principle would never have occurred to him. The vine was the gift of God. Prefer nothing to it for planting in the

[55]

mellow soil of Tibur, Varus; it is one of the compensations of life:

> " I*ts magic power of wit can spread*
> T*he halo round a dullard's head,*
> C*an make the sage forget his care,*
> H*is bosom's inmost thoughts unbare,*
> A*nd drown his solemn-faced pretense*
> B*eneath its blithesome influence.*
> B*right hope it brings and vigor back*
> T*o minds outworn upon the rack,*
> A*nd puts such courage in the brain*
> A*s makes the poor be men again,*
> W*hom neither tyrants' wrath affrights,*
> N*or all their bristling satellites.*"

When wine is a curse, it is not so because of itself, but because of excess in its use. The cup was made for purposes of pleasure, but to quarrel over it, — leave that to barbarians! Take warning by the Thracians, and the Centaurs and Lapiths, never to overstep the bounds of moderation. Pleasure with after-taste of bitterness is not real pleasure. Pleasure purchased with pain is an evil.

Upon women he looks with the same philosophic calm as upon wine. Love, too, was to be regarded as one of the contributions to life's pleasure. To dally with golden-haired Pyrrha, with Lyce, or with Glycera, the beauty more brilliant than Parian marble, was not in his eyes to be blamed in itself. What he felt no hesitation in committing to his poems for friends and the Emperor to read, they on their part felt as little hesitation in confessing to him. The fault of love lay not in itself, but in abuse. This is not said of adultery, which was always an offense because it disturbed the institution of marriage and rotted the foundation of society.

There is thus no inconsistency in the Horace of the love poems and the Horace of the *Secular Hymn* who petitions Our Lady Juno to prosper the decrees of the Senate encouraging the marriage relation and the rearing of families. Of the illicit love that looked to Roman women in the home, he emphatically declares his innocence, and against it directs the last and most powerful of the six *Inaugural Odes;* for this touched the family, and, through the family, the State. This, with neglect of religion, he classes together as the two great causes of national decay.

Horace is not an Ovid, with no sense of the limits of either indulgence or expression. He is not a Catullus, tormented by the furies of youthful passion. The flame never really burned him. We search his pages in vain for evidence of sincere and absorbing passion, whether of the flesh or of the spirit. He was guilty of no breach of the morals of his time, and it is likely also, in spite of Suetonius, that he was guilty of no excess. He was a supporter in good faith of the Emperor in his attempts at the moral improvement of the State. If Virgil in the writing of the *Georgics* or the *Aeneid* was conscious of a purpose to second the project of Augustus, it is just as likely that his intimate friend Horace also wrote with conscious moral intent. Nothing is more in keeping with his conception of the end and effect of literature:

It shapes the tender and hesitating speech of the child; it straight removes his ear from shameless communication; presently with friendly precepts it moulds his inner self; it is a corrector of harshness and envy and anger; it sets forth the righteous deed; it instructs the rising generations with the familiar example; it is a solace to the helpless and the sick at heart.

Horace's philosophy of life is thus based upon something deeper than the principle of seizing upon pleasure. His definition of pleasure is not without austerity; he preaches the positive virtues of performance as well as the negative virtue of moderation. He could be an unswerving follower and guardian of true virtue, and could bend self to circumstance.

He stands for domestic purity, and for patriotic devotion. *Dulce et decorum est pro patria mori,* — to die for country is a privilege and a glory. His hero is Regulus, returning steadfastly through the ranks of protesting friends to keep faith with the pitiless executioners of Carthage. Regulus, and the Scauri, and Paulus, who poured out his great spirit on the disastrous field of Cannae, and Fabricius, of simple heart and absolute integrity, he holds up as examples to his generation. In praise of the sturdy Roman qualities of courage and steadfastness he writes his most inspired lines:

The righteous man of unswerving purpose is shaken in his solid will neither by the unworthy demands of inflamed citizens, nor by the frowning face of the threatening tyrant, nor by the East-wind, turbid ruler of the restless Adriatic, nor by the great hand of fulminating Jove himself. If the heavens should fall asunder, the crashing fragments would descend upon him unterrified.

He preaches the gospel of faithfulness not only to family, country, and purpose, but to religion. He will shun the man who violates the secrets of the mysteries. The curse of the gods is upon all such, and pursues them to the day of doom.

Faithfulness to friendship stands out with no less distinctness. While Horace is in his right mind, he will value nothing so highly as a delightful friend. He is ready, whenever fate calls, to enter with Maecenas even upon the last journey. Among the blest is he who is unafraid to die for dear friends or native land.

Honor, too, — the fine spirit of old Roman times, that refused bribes, that would not take advantage of an enemy's weakness, that asked no questions save the question of what was right, that never turned its back upon duty, that swore to its own hurt and changed not; the same lofty spirit the recording of whose manifestations never fails to bring the glow to

Livy's cheek and the gleam to his eye, —
honor is also first and foremost in Horace's
esteem. Regulus, the self-sacrificing; Curius,
despising the Samnite gold; Camillus, yielding
private grievance to come to his country's aid;
Cato, dying for his convictions after Thapsus,
are his inspirations. The hero of his ideal fears
disgrace worse than death. The diadem and
the laurel are for him only who can pass on
without the backward glance upon stores of
treasure.

Finally, not least among the qualities which
enter into the ideal of Horace is the simplicity
of the olden time, when the armies of Rome
were made up of citizen-soldiers, and the eye
of every Roman was single to the glory of
the State, and the selfishness of luxury was yet
unknown.

Scant were their private means, the public, great;
'Twas still a commonwealth, that State;
No portico, surveyed with private rule,
Assured one man the shady cool.

The laws approved the house of humble sods;
'Twas only to the homes of gods,
The structures reared with earnings of the nation,
They gave rich marble decoration.

The healthful repose of heart which comes from unity of purpose and simple devotion to plain duty, he sees existing still, even in his own less strenuous age, in the remote and peaceful countryside. Blessed is the man far from the busy life of affairs, like the primeval race of mortals, who tills with his own oxen the acres of his fathers! Horace covets the gift earnestly for himself, because his calm vision assures him that it, of all the virtues, lies next to happy living.

v. THE SOURCES OF HAPPINESS

Here we have arrived at the kernel of Horace's philosophy, the key which unlocks the casket containing his message to all men of every generation. In actual life, at least, mankind storms the citadel of happiness, as if it were something material and external, to be taken by violent hands. Horace locates the citadels of happiness in his own breast. It is the heart which is the source of all joy and all sorrow, of all wealth and all poverty. Happiness is to be sought, not outside, but within. Man does not create his world; he *is* his world.

Men are madly chasing after peace of heart

in a thousand wrong ways, all the while over-
looking the right way, which is nearest at hand.
To observe their feverish eagerness, the spectator might be led to think happiness identical
with possession. And yet wealth and happiness are neither the same nor equivalent.
They may have nothing to do one with the
other. Money, indeed, is not an evil in itself,
but it is not essential except so far as it is a
mere means of life. Poor men may be happy,
and the wealthy may be poor in the midst of
their riches. A man's wealth consisteth not in
the abundance of the things he possesseth.
More justly does he lay claim to the name of
rich man who knows how to use the blessings
of the gods wisely, who is bred to endurance
of hard want, and who fears the disgraceful
action worse than he fears death.

Real happiness consists in peace of mind
and heart. Everyone desires it, and everyone
prays for it, — the sailor caught in the storms
of the Aegean, the mad Thracian, the Mede
with quiver at his back. But peace is not to
be purchased. Neither gems nor purple nor
gold will buy it, nor favor. Not all the externals in the world can help the man who depends
upon them alone.

[63]

Not treasure trove nor consul's stately train
Drives wretched tumult from the troubled brain;
Swarming with cares that draw unceasing sighs,
The fretted ceiling hangs o'er sleepless eyes.

Nor is peace to be pursued and laid hold of, or discovered in some other clime. Of what avail to fly to lands warmed by other suns? What exile ever escaped himself? It is the soul that is at fault, that never can be freed from its own bonds. The sky is all he changes:

The heavens, not themselves, they change
Who haste to cross the seas.

The happiness men seek for is in themselves, to be found at little Ulubrae in the Latin marshes as easily as in great cities, if only they have the proper attitude of mind and heart.

But how insure this peace of mind?

At the very beginning, and through to the end, the searcher after happiness must recognize that unhappiness is the result of slavery of some sort, and that slavery in turn is begotten of desire. The man who is overfond of anything will be unwilling to let go his hold upon it. Desire will curb his freedom. The only safety lies in refusing the rein to passion of any kind. " To gaze upon nothing to lust after it, Numicius, is the simple way of winning and of keeping happiness." He who lives in either desire or fear can never enjoy his possessions. He who desires will also fear; and he who fears can never be a free man. The wise man will not allow his desires to become tyrants over him. Money will be his servant, not his master. He will attain to wealth by curbing his wants. You will be monarch over broader realms by dominating your spirit than by adding Libya to far-off Gades.

The poor man, in spite of poverty, may enjoy life more than the rich. It is possible under a humble roof to excel in happiness kings and the friends of kings. Wealth depends upon what men want, not upon what men have. The more a man denies himself, the greater are the gifts of the gods to him. One may hold riches in contempt, and thus be a more splendid lord of wealth than the great landowner of Apulia. By contracting his desires he may extend his revenues until they are more than those of the gorgeous East. Many wants attend those who have many ambitions. Happy is the man to whom God has given barely enough. Let him to whom fate, fortune, or his own effort has given this enough, desire no more. If the liquid stream of Fortune should gild him, it would make his happiness nothing greater, because money cannot change his nature. To the man who has good digestion and good lungs and is free from gout, the riches of a king could add nothing. What difference does it make to him who lives within the limits of nature whether he plow a hundred acres or a thousand?

As with the passion of greed, so with anger, love, ambition for power, and all the other forms of desire which lodge in the human heart. Make them your slaves, or they will make you theirs. Like wrath, they are all forms of madness. The man who becomes avaricious has thrown away the armor of life, has abandoned the post of virtue. Once let a man submit to desire of an unworthy kind, and he will find himself in the case of the horse that called a rider to help him drive the stag from their common feeding-ground, and received the bit and rein forever.

So Horace will enter into no entangling alliances with ambition for power, wealth, or position, or with the more personal passions. By some of them he has not been altogether untouched, and he has no regret; but to continue, at forty-five, would not do. He will be content with just his home in the Sabine hills. This is what he always prayed for, a patch of ground, not so very large, with a spring of ever-flowing water, a garden, and a little timberland. He asks for nothing more, except that a kindly fate will make these beloved possessions forever his own. He will go to the ant, for she is an example, and consider her ways and be wise, and be content with what he has as soon as it is enough. He will not enter the field of public life, because it would mean the sacrifice of peace. He would have to keep open house, submit to the attentions of a bodyguard of servants, keep horses and carriage and a coachman, and be the target for shafts of envy and malice; in a word, lose his freedom and become the slave of wretched and burdensome ambition.

The price is too great, the privilege not to his liking. Horace's prayer is rather to be freed from the cares of empty ambition, from the fear of death and the passion of anger, to laugh at superstition, to enjoy the happy return of his birthday, to be forgiving of his friends, to grow more gentle and better as old age draws on, to recognize the proper limit in all things:

> " *Health to enjoy the blessings sent*
>   *From heaven; a mind unclouded, strong;*
> *A cheerful heart; a wise content;*
>   *An honored age; and song.*"

II. HORACE THROUGH THE AGES

Introductory

THUS much we have had to say in the interpretation of Horace. Our interpretation has centered about his qualities as a person: his broad experience, his sensitiveness, his responsiveness, his powers of assimilation, his gift of expression, his concreteness as a representative of the world of culture, as a son of Italy, as a citizen of eternal Rome, as a member of the universal human family.

Let us now tell the story of Horace in the life of after times. It will include an account of the esteem in which he was held while still in the flesh; of the fame he enjoyed and the influence he exercised until Rome as a great empire was no more and the Roman tongue and Roman spirit alike were decayed; of the way in which his works were preserved intact through obscure centuries of ignorance and turmoil; and of their second birth when men began to delight once more in the luxuries of the mind. This will prepare the way for a final chapter, on the peculiar quality and manner of the Horatian influence.

1. HORACE THE PROPHET

HORACE is aware of his qualities as a poet. In an interesting blend, of which the first and larger part is detached and judicial estimation of his work, a second part literary convention, and the third and least a smiling and inoffensive self-assertion, he prophesies his own immortality.

From infancy he has been set apart as the child of the Muses. At birth Melpomene marked him for her own. The doves of ancient story covered him over with the green leaves of the Apulian wood as, lost and overcome by weariness, he lay in peaceful slumber, and kept him safe from creeping and four-footed things, a babe secure in the favor of heaven. The sacred charm that rests upon him preserved him in the rout at Philippi, rescued him from the Sabine wolf, saved him from death by the falling tree and the waters of shipwreck. He will abide under its shadow wherever he may go, — to his favorite haunts in Latium, to the

far north where fierce Britons offer up the
stranger to their gods, to the far east and the
blazing sands of the Syrian desert, to rude
Spain and the streams of Scythia, to the tree-
less, naked fields of the frozen pole, to home-
less lands under the fiery car of the too-near
sun. He will rise superior to the envy of men.
The pinions that bear him aloft through the
clear ether will be of no usual or flagging sort.
For him there shall be no death, no Stygian
wave across which none returns:

Forego the dirge; let no one raise the cry,
  Or make unseemly show of grief and gloom,
Nor think o'er me, who shall not really die,
  To rear the empty honor of the tomb.

His real self will remain among men, ever
springing afresh in their words of praise:

Not lasting bronze nor pyramid upreared
By princes shall outlive my powerful rhyme.
The monument I build, to men endeared,
Not biting rain, nor raging wind, nor time,
Endlessly flowing through the countless years,
Shall e'er destroy. I shall not wholly die;
The grave shall have of me but what appears;
For me fresh praise shall ever multiply.

[71]

As long as priest and silent Vestal wind
The Capitolian steep, tongues shall tell o'er
How humble Horace rose above his kind
Where Aufidus's rushing waters roar
In the parched land where rustic Daunus reigned,
And first taught Grecian numbers how to run
In Latin measure. Muse! the honor gained
Is thine, for I am thine till time is done.
Gracious Melpomene, O hear me now,
And with the Delphic bay gird round my brow.

Yet Horace does not always refer to his poetry in this serious vein; if indeed we are to call serious a manner of literary prophecy which has always been more or less conventional. His frequent disclaimers of the higher inspiration are well known. The Muse forbids him to attempt the epic strain or the praise of Augustus and Agrippa. In the face of grand themes like these, his genius is slight. He will not essay even the strain of Simonides in the lament for an Empire stained by land and sea with the blood of fratricidal war. His themes shall be rather the feast and the mimic battles of revelling youths and maidens, the making of love in the grots of Venus. His lyre shall be jocose, his plectrum of the lighter sort.

He not only half-humorously disclaims the

capacity for lofty themes, but, especially as he grows older and more philosophic, and perhaps less lyric, half-seriously attributes whatever he does to persevering effort.   He has

> *"Nor the pride nor ample pinion*
> *That the Theban eagle bear,*
> *Sailing with supreme dominion*
> *Through the azure deep of air;"*

he is the bee, with infinite industry flitting from flower to flower, the unpretending maker of verse, fashioning his songs with only toil and patience.   He believes in the file, in long delay before giving forth to the world the poem that henceforth can never be recalled.   The only inspiration he claims for *Satire* and *Epistle,* which, he says, approximate the style of spoken discourse, lies in the aptness and patience with which he fashions his verses from language in ordinary use, giving to words new dignity by means of skillful combination.   Let anyone who wishes to be convinced undertake to do the same; he will find himself perspiring in a vain attempt.

And if Horace did not always conceive of his inspiration as purely ethereal, neither did he always dream of the path to immortality

as leading through the spacious reaches of the
upper air. At forty-four, he is already
aware of a more pedestrian path. He
has observed the ways of the public with
literature, as any writer must observe
them still, and knows also of a certain
use to which his poems are being put. Perhaps
with some secret pride, but surely with a philosophic resignation that is like good-humored
despair, he sees that the path is pedagogical.
In reproachful tones, he addresses the book of
Epistles that is so eager to try its fortune in
the big world: But if the prophet is not
blinded by disgust at your foolishness, you will
be prized at Rome until the charm of youth has
left you. Then, soiled and worn by much
handling of the common crowd, you will either
silently give food to vandal worms, or seek
exile in Utica, or be tied up and sent to Ilerda.
The monitor you did not heed will laugh, like
the man who sent his balky ass headlong over
the cliff; for who would trouble to save anyone against his will? This lot, too, you may
expect: for a stammering old age to come upon
you teaching children to read in the out-of-the-
way parts of town.

2. HORACE AND ANCIENT ROME

THAT Horace refers to being pointed out by the passer-by as the minstrel of the Roman lyre, or, in other words, as the laureate, that his satire provokes sufficient criticism to draw from him a defense and a justification of himself against the charge of cynicism, and that he finally records a greater freedom from the tooth of envy, are all indications of the prominence to which he rose. That Virgil and Varius, poets of recognized worth, and their friend Plotius Tucca, third of the whitest souls of earth, introduced him to the attention of Maecenas, and that the discriminating lover of excellence became his patron and made him known to Augustus, are evidences of the appeal of which he was capable both as poet and man. In the many names of worthy and distinguished men of letters and affairs to whom he addresses the individual poems, and with whom he must therefore have been on terms of mutual respect, is seen a further proof. Even Virgil contains passages disclosing a more than ordinary familiarity with Horace's work, and men like Ovid and Propertius, of whose personal relations with Horace nothing is known, not only knew but absorbed his poems.

If still further evidence of Horace's worth is required, it may be seen in his being invited to commemorate the exploits of Drusus and Tiberius, the royal stepsons, against the hordes of the North, and the greatness of Augustus himself, ever-present help of Italy, and imperial Rome; and in the Emperor's expression of disappointment, sometime before the second book of *Epistles* was published, that he had been mentioned in none of the " Talks." And, finally, if there remained in the minds of his generation any shadow of doubt as to the esteem in which he was held by the foremost men in the State, who were in most cases men of letters as well as patrons of letters, it was dispelled when, in the year 17, Horace was chosen to write the *Secular Hymn*, for use in the greatest religious and patriotic festival of the times.

These facts receive greater significance from an appreciation of the poet's sincerity and independence. He will restore to Maecenas his gifts, if their possession is to mean a curb upon the freedom of living his nature calls for. He declines a secretaryship to the Emperor himself, and without offense to his imperial friend, who bids him be free of his house as if it were his own.

But Horace must submit also to the more impartial judgment of time. Of the two innovations which gave him relief against the general background, one was the amplification of the crude but vigorous satire of Lucilius into a more perfect literary character, and the other was the persuasion of the Greek lyric forms into Roman service. Both examples had their important effects within the hundred years that followed on Horace's death.

The satire and epistle, which Horace hardly distinguished, giving to both the name of *Sermo,* or " Talk," was the easier to imitate. Persius, dying in the year 62, at the age of twenty-eight, was steeped in Horace, but lacked the gentle spirit, the genial humor, and the suavity of expression that make Horatian satire a delight. In Juvenal, writing under Trajan and Hadrian, the tendency of satire toward consistent aggressiveness which is present in Horace and further advanced in Persius, has reached its goal. With Juvenal, satire is a matter of the lash, of vicious cut and thrust. Juvenal may tell the

truth, but the smiling face of Horatian satire
has disappeared. With him the line of Roman
satire is extinct, but the nature of satire for all
time to come is fixed. Juvenal, employing the
form of Horace and substituting for his content of mellow contentment and good humor
the bitterness of an outraged moral sense, is
the last Roman and the first modern satirist.

The *Odes* found more to imitate them, but
none to rival. The most pronounced example
of their influence is found in the choruses of
the tragic poet Seneca, where form and substance alike are constantly reminiscent of
Horace. Two comments on the *Odes* from the
second half of the first century are of even
greater eloquence than Seneca's example as
testimonials to the impression made by the
Horatian lyric. Petronius, of Nero's time,
speaks of the poet's *curiosa felicitas,* meaning
the gift of arriving, by long and careful search,
at the inevitable word or phrase. Quintilian,
writing his treatise on Instruction, sums him
up thus: " Of our lyric poets, Horace is about
the only one worth reading; for he sometimes
reaches real heights, and he is at the same time
full of delightfulness and grace, and both in
variety of imagery and in words is most hap-

[78]

pily daring." To these broad strokes the modern critic has added little except by way of elaboration.

The *Life of Horace,* written by Suetonius, the secretary of Hadrian, contains evidence of another, and perhaps a stronger, character regarding the poet's power. We see that doubtful imitations are beginning to circulate. " I possess," says the imperial secretary, " some elegies attributed to his pen, and a letter in prose, supposed to be a recommendation of himself to Maecenas, but I think that both are spurious; for the elegies are commonplace, and the letter is, besides, obscure, which was by no means one of his faults."

The history of Roman literature from the end of the first century after Christ is the story of the decline of inspiration, the decline of taste, the decline of language, the decline of intellectual interest. Beneath it all and through it all there is spreading, gradually and silently, the insidious decay that will surely crumble the constitution of the ancient world. Pagan letters are uncreative, and, with few exceptions, without imagination and dull. The literature of the new religion, beginning to push green shoots from the ruins of the times, is a mingling of old and new substance under forms that are always old.

In the main, neither Christian nor pagan will be attracted by Horace. The Christian will see in his gracious resignation only the philosophy of despair, and in his light humors only careless indulgence in the vanities of this world and blindness to the eternal concerns of life. The pagan will not appreciate the delicacy of his art, and will find the abundance of his literary, mythological, historical, and geographical allusion, the compactness of his expression, and the maturity and depth of his intellect, a barrier calling for too much effort. Both will prefer Virgil, — Virgil of " arms and the man," the story-teller, Virgil the lover of Italy, Virgil the glorifier of Roman deeds and destiny, Virgil the readily understood, Virgil who has already drawn aside, at least partly, the veil that hangs before the mystic otherworld, Virgil the almost Christian prophet, with the almost Biblical language, Virgil the spiritual, Virgil the comforter.

Horace will not be popular. He will remain the poet of the few who enjoy the process of thinking and recognize the charm of skillful expression. Tacitus and Juvenal esteem him, the Emperor Alexander Severus reads him in leisure hours, the long list of mediocrities representing the course of literary history demonstrate by their content that the education of men of letters in general includes a knowledge of him. The greatest of the late pagans, — Ausonius and Claudian at the end of the fourth century; Boëthius, philosopher-victim of Theodoric in the early sixth; Cassiodorus, the chronicler, imperial functionary in the same century, — disclose a familiarity whose foundations are to be looked for in love and enthusiasm rather than in mere cultivation. It may be safely assumed that, in general, appreciation of Horace was proportionate to greatness of soul and real love of literature.

The same assumption may be made in the realm of Christian literature. Minucius Felix, calmly and logically arguing the case of Christianity against paganism, Tertullian the fiery preacher, Cyprian the enthusiast and martyr, Arnobius the rhetorical, contain no indications of familiarity with Horace, though this is not conclusive proof that they did not know and admire him; but Lactantius, the Christian Cicero, Jerome, the sympathetic, the sensitive,

[81]

the intense, the irascible, Prudentius, the most
original and the most vigorous of the Christian
poets, and even Venantius Fortunatus, bishop
and traveler in the late sixth century, and last
of the Christian poets while Latin was still a
native tongue, display a knowledge of Horace
which argues also a love for him.

The name of Venantius Fortunatus brings
us to the very brink of the centuries called the
Middle Age. If there are those who object
to the name of Dark Age as doing injustice to
the life of the times, they must at any rate
agree that for Horace it was really dark. That
his light was not totally lost in the shadows
which enveloped the art of letters was due to
one aspect of his immortality which we must
notice before leaving the era of ancient Rome.

Thus far, in accounting for Horace's continued fame, we have considered only his
appeal to the individual intellect and taste, the
admiration which represented an interest spontaneous and sincere. There was another phase
of his fame which expressed an interest less
inspired, though its first cause was none the
less in the enthusiasm of the elect. It was the
phase foreseen by Horace himself, and its first
manifestations had probably appeared in his

own life-time. It was the immortality of the
text-book and the commentary.

Quintilian's estimate of Horace in the *Insti-
tutes* is an indication that the poet was already
a subject of school instruction in the latter half
of the first century. Juvenal, in the first
quarter of the next, gives us a chiaroscuro
glimpse into a Roman school-interior where
little boys are sitting at their desks in early
morning, each with odorous lamp shining upon
school editions of Horace and Virgil smudged
and discolored by soot from the wicks,

> *totidem olfecisse lucernas,*
> *Quot stabant pueri, cum totus decolor esset*
> *Flaccus et haereret nigro fuligo Maroni.*
> (VII. 225 ff.)

The use of the poet in the schools meant that
lovers of learning as well as lovers of literary
art were occupying themselves with Horace.
The first critical edition of his works, by
Marcus Valerius Probus, appeared as early as
the time of Nero. A native of Berytus, the
modern Beirut, disappointed in the military
career, he turned to the collection, study, and
critical editing of Latin authors, among whom,
besides Horace, were Virgil, Lucretius, Persius,

and Terence. His method, comprising careful comparison of manuscripts, emendations, and punctuation, with annotations explanatory and aesthetic, all prefaced by the author's biography, won him the reputation of the most erudite of Roman men of letters. It is in no small measure due to him that the tradition of Horace's text is so comparatively good.

There were many other critics and interpreters of Horace. Of many of them, the names as well as the works have been lost. Modestus and Claranus, perhaps not long after Probus, are two names that survive. Suetonius, as we have seen, wrote the poet's *Life,* though it contains almost nothing not found in the works of Horace themselves. In the time of Hadrian appeared also the edition of Quintus Terentius Scaurus, in ten books, of which the *Odes* and *Epodes* made five, and the *Satires* and *Epistles* five, the *Ars Poetica* being set apart as a book in itself. At the end of the second or the beginning of the third century, Helenius Acro wrote commentaries on certain plays of Terence and on Horace, giving special attention to the persons appearing in the poet's pages, a favorite subject on which a considerable body of writing sprang up. Not long afterward ap-

peared the commentary of Pomponius Porphyrio, originally published with the text of
Horace, but later separately. In spite of
modifications wrought in the course of time,
only Porphyrio's, of all the commentaries of
the first three hundred years, has preserved an
approximation to its original character and
quantity. Acro's has been overlaid by other
commentators until the identity of his work is
lost. The purpose of Porphyrio was to bring
poetic beauty into relief by clarifying construc-
tion and sense, rather than to engage in learned
exposition of the subject matter.

Finally, in the year 527, the consul Vettius
Agorius Basilius Mavortius, with the collabo-
ration of one Felix, revised the text of at least
the *Odes* and *Epodes,* and perhaps also of the
Satires and *Epistles*. That there were many
other editions intervening between Porphyrio's
and his, there can be little doubt.

This review of scant and scattered, but consistent, evidence is proof enough of Horace's
hold upon the intellectual and literary leaders
of the ancient Roman world. For the individual pagan who clung to the old order, he
represented more acceptably than anyone else,
or anyone else but Virgil, the ideal of a glorious

[85]

past, and afforded consequently something of inspiration for the decaying present. Upon men who, whether pagan or Christian, were possessed by literary enthusiasms, and upon men who delighted in contemplation of the human kind, he cast the spell of art and humanity. Those who caught the fire directly may indeed have been few, but they were men of parts whose fire was communicated.

As for the influence exercised by Horace upon Roman society at large through generation after generation of schoolboys as the centuries passed, its depth and breadth cannot be measured. It may be partly appreciated, however, by those who realize from their own experience both as pupils and teachers the effect upon growing and impressionable minds of a literature rich in morality and patriotism, and who reflect upon the greater amplitude of literary instruction among the ancients, by whom a Homer, a Virgil, or a Horace was made the vehicle of discipline so broad and varied as to be an education in itself.

3. Horace and the Middle Age

THERE is no such thing as a line marking definitely the time when ancient Rome ceased to be itself and became the Rome of the Middle Age. If there were such a line, we should probably have crossed it already, whether in recording the last real Roman setting of the Horatian house in order by Mavortius in 527, or in referring to Venantius Fortunatus, the last of the Latin Christian poets. The usual date marking the end of the Western Empire, 476, is only the convenient sign for the culmination of the movement long since begun in the interferences of an army composed more and more of a non-Italian, Northern soldiery, and ending in a final mutiny or revolt which assumed the character of invasion and the permanent seizure of civil as well as military authority. The coming of Odoacer is the ultimate stage in the process of Roman and Italian exhaustion, the sign that life is not longer possible except through infusion of northern blood.

The military and political change itself was only exterior, the outward demonstration of deep-seated maladies. The too-successful bureaucratization of Augustus and such of his successors as were really able and virtuous, the development of authority into tyranny by such as were neither able nor virtuous, but mad and wilful, had removed from Roman citizenship the responsibility which in the olden time had made it strong; and the increase of taxes, assessments, and compulsory honors involving personal contribution, had substituted for responsibility and privilege a burden so heavy that under it the civic life of the Empire was crushed to extinction. In Italy, above all, the ancient seed was running out. Under the influence of economic and social movement, the old stock had died and disappeared, or changed beyond recognition. The old language, except in the mouths and from the pens of the few, was fast losing its identity. Uncertainty, indifference, stagnation, weariness of body, mind, and soul, leaden resignation and despair, forgetfulness of the glories of the past in art and even in heroism, were the inheritance of the last generations of the old order. Jerome felt barbarism closing in: *Romanus orbis ruit,* he says, — the Roman world is tumbling in ruins.

In measure as the vitality of pagan Rome was sapped, into the inert and decaying mass there penetrated gradually the two new life-currents of a new religion and a new blood. The change they wrought from the first century to the descent of the Northerners was not sudden, nor was it rapid. Nor was it always a change that carried visible warrant of virtue. The mingling of external races in the army and in trade, the interference of a Northern soldiery in the affairs of the throne, the more peaceful but more intimate shuffling of the population through the social and economic emergence of the one-time nameless and poor, whether of native origin or foreign, may have contributed fresh blood to an anaemic society, but the result most apparent to the eye and most disturbing to the soul was the debasement of standards and the fears that naturally come with violent, sudden, or merely unfamiliar change. The new religion may have contributed new hope and erected new standards, but it also contributed exaggerations, contradictions, and new uncertainties. The life of logic began to be displaced by the life of feeling.

The change and turmoil of the times that attended and followed the crumbling of the Roman world were favorable neither to the production of letters nor to the enjoyment of a literary heritage. Goth, Byzantine, Lombard, Frank, German, Saracen, and Norman made free of the soil of Italy. If men were not without leisure, they were without the leisure of peaceful and careful contemplation, and lacked the buoyant heart without which assimilation of art is hardly less possible than creation. Ignorance had descended upon the world, and gross darkness covered the people. The classical authors were solid, the meat of vigorous minds. Their language, never the facile language of the people and the partially disciplined, now became a resisting medium that was foreign to the general run of men. Their syntax was archaic and crabbed, their metres forgotten. Their substance, never grasped without effort, was now not only difficult, but became the abstruse matter of another people and another age. To all but the cultivated few, they were known for anything but what they really were. It was an age of Virgil the mysterious prophet of the coming of Christ, of Virgil the necromancer. Real knowledge withdrew to secret and secluded refuges.

If the classical authors in general were beyond the powers and outside the affection of men, Horace was especially so. More intellectual than Virgil, and less emotional, in metrical forms for the most part lost to their knowledge and liking, the poet of the individual heart rather than of men in the national or racial mass, the poet strictly of this world and in no respect of the next, he almost vanished from the life of men.

Yet the classics were not all lost, and not even Horace perished. Strange to say, and yet not really strange, the most potent active influence in the destruction of his appeal to men was also the most effective instrument of his preservation. Through the darkness and the storms of the nine hundred years following the fall of the Western Empire, Horace was sheltered under the wing of the Church.

It was a natural exaggeration for Christianity to begin by teaching absolute separation from the world, and to declare, through the mouths of such as Tertullian, that the blood of Christ alone sufficed and nothing more was needed, and that literature and all the other arts of paganism, together with its manners, were so inseparable from its religion that every part was anathema. It was natural that Horace, more than Virgil, should be the object of its neglect, and even of its active enmity. Horace is the most completely pagan of poets whose works are of spiritual import. The only immortality of which he takes account is the immortality of fame. Aside from this, the end of man is dust and shadow.

It is true that in the depth of his heart he does not feel with Democritus, Epicurus, and Lucretius that " Dust thou art, to dust returnest " is spoken of soul as well as body. The old Roman instinct for ancestor-communion is too strong in him for that. But he acquiesces in their doctrine in so far as shadowy existence in another world inspires in him no pleasing hope. He displays no trace of the faith in the supernatural which accompanies the Christian hope of happy immortality. He contains none of the expressions of yearning for communion with the divine, of self-abasement in the presence of the eternal, which belong to Christian poetry. The flights of his muse rarely take him into the realm of a divine love and providence. His aspirations are for things achievable in this world: for faithfulness in friendship, for enduring courage, for irreproachable patriotism, — in short, for ideal *human* relations.

Horace's idealism is not Christian idealism, and is only in a limited way even spiritual idealism. When he prays, it is likely to be for others rather than himself, and for temporal blessings only: for the success of Augustus at home and in the field, for prolongation of Maecenas' life and happiness, for the weal of the State, for the nurslings of his little flock, for health of body and contentment of heart. His dwelling is not in the secret place of the Most High. Philosophy, not religion, is his refuge and his fortress. In philosophy, not in God, will he trust.

In a word, Horace is logical, self-reliant, and self-sufficient. He sees no happy future after this life, is conscious of no providence watching over him, is involved in no obligation to the beings of an eternal world. He looks this world and the next, gods and men, directly in the face, and expects other men to do the same. Life and its duties are for him clear-cut. He is no propounder of problems, no searcher after hidden purposes. He lacks almost absolutely the feverish aspiration and unrest which characterize Christian and other humanitarian modes of thought and sentiment, and whose manifestation is one of the best known features

of recent modern times, as it was of the earliest
Christian experience.

But Christianity was a religion of men, and
therefore human. If its exaggerations were
natural, its reservations and its reactions were
also natural. There were men whose admiration continued to be roused and whose affections
continued to be touched by Virgil and Horace.
There were men whose reason as well as whose
instinct impelled them to employ the classic
authors and the classic arts in the service of the
new religion. Christianity possessed no distinct and separate media of expression and no
separate body of knowledge which could bear
fruit as matter of instruction. Pagan art and
literature were indispensable whether for the
study of history or of mere humanity. Christianity was therefore compelled to employ the
old forms of art, which involved the use of
the old instrumentalities of literary education. When, finally, paganism had fallen
under its repeated assaults, what had been
forced use became a matter of choice,
and the classics were taken under the
Church's protection and marked with her
approval.

The data regarding Horace in the Middle

Age are few, but they are clear. We need not examine them all in order to draw conclusions.

The monastic idea, of eastern origin and given currency in the West by Jerome, was first reduced to systematic practice by Benedict, who created the first Rule at Monte Cassino about the time of the Mavortian recension of Horace, in 527. New moral strength issued from the cloisters now rapidly established. Cassiodorus, especially active in promoting the spiritual phase of monkish retreat, made the intellectual life also his concern. Monte Cassino, between Naples and Rome, and Bobbio, in the northern part of the peninsula, were the great Italian centers. The Benedictine influence spread to Ireland, which before the end of the sixth century became a stronghold of the movement and an inspiration to England, Germany, France, and even Italy, where Bobbio itself was founded by Columban and his companions. St. Gall in Switzerland, Fulda at Hersfeld in Hesse-Nassau, Corvey in Saxony, Iona in Scotland, Tours in France, Reichenau on Lake Constance, were all active centers of religion and learning within two hundred years from Benedict's death.

The monasteries not only afforded the spiritual enthusiast the opportunity of separation from the world of temptation and storm, but were equally inviting to men devoted first of all to the intellectual life. The scholar and the educator found within their walls not only peaceful escape from the harshnesses of political change and military broil, but the opportunity to labor usefully and unmolested in the occupation that pleased them most. The cloister became a Christian institute. The example of Cassiodorus was followed two hundred years later on a larger scale by Charlemagne. Schools were founded both in cloister and at court, scholars summoned, manuscripts copied, the life of pagan antiquity studied, and the bond between the languages and cultures of present and past made firmer. The schools of the old régime had fallen away in the sixth century, when Northern rule had closed the civic career to natives of Italy. A great advance in the intellectual life now laid the foundations of all cultural effort in the Middle Age.

No small part of this advance was due to the preservation of manuscripts by copying. In this activity France was first, so far as Horace was concerned. The copies by the scribes of Charlemagne went back to Mavortius and Porphyrio, the originals of which were probably discovered at Bobbio by his scholars. Of the two hundred and fifty manuscripts in existence, the greater part are French in origin, the oldest being the Bernensis, of the ninth or tenth century, from near Orléans. Germany was a worthy second to France. The finds in monastery libraries of both countries in the humanist movement of the fifteenth century were especially rich. Italy, on the contrary, preserved few manuscripts of her poet, and none that is really ancient. Italy began the great monastery movement, but disorder and change were against the diffusion of culture. Charlemagne's efforts probably had little to do with Italy. The Church seems to have had no care to preserve the ancient culture of her native land.

What this meant in terms of actual acquaintance with the poet would not be clear without evidence of other kinds. By the end of the sixth century, knowledge of Horace was already vague. He was not read in Africa, Spain, or Gaul. Read in Italy up to Charlemagne's time, a hundred years later his works are not to be found in the catalogue of Bobbio, one of the greatest seats of learning. What the general attitude of the Church's leadership toward him was, may be conjectured from the declaration of Gregory the Great against all beauty in writing. Its general capacity for Horace may perhaps be surmised also from the confession of the Pope's contemporary, Gregory of Tours, that he is unfamiliar with the ancient literary languages. The few readers of the late Empire had become fewer still. The difficult form and matter of the *Odes,* and their unadaptability to religious and moral use, disqualified them for the approval of all but the individual scholar or literary enthusiast. The moralities of the *Epistles* were more tractable, and formed the largest contribution to the *Florilegia,* or flower-collections, that were circulated by themselves. Horace did not contain the facile and stimulating tales of Ovid, he was not a Virgil the story-teller and almost Christian, his lines did not exercise a strong appeal to the ear, he was not an example of the rhetorical, like Lucan, his satire did not lend itself, like a Juvenal's, to universal condemnation of paganism.

In the eighth century, Columban knows Horace, the Venerable Bede cites him four times, and Alcuin is called a Flaccus. The

York catalogue of Alcuin shows the presence of most of the classic authors. Paul the Deacon, who wrote a poem in the Sapphics he learned from Horace, is declared, he says, to be like Homer, Flaccus, and Virgil, but ungratefully and ungraciously adds, "men like that I'll compare with dogs." In Spain, Saint Isidore of Seville knew Horace in the seventh century, though the Rule of Isidore, as of some other monastic legislators, forbade the use of pagan authors without special permission; yet the coming of the Arabs in the eighth century, and the struggle between the Gothic, Christian, and Islamic civilizations resulted, for the next six or seven centuries, in what seems total oblivion of the poet.

In the ninth and tenth centuries, under the impulse of the Carolingian favor, France, in which there is heretofore no evidence of Horace's presence from the end of Roman times, becomes the greatest center of manuscript activity, the Bernensis and six Parisian exemplars dating from this period. Yet the indexes of St. Gall, Reichenau, and Bobbio contain the name of no work of Horace, and only Nevers and Loesch contained his complete works. The *Ecbasis Captivi,* an animal-

epic appearing at Toul in 940, has one fifth of
its verses formed out of Horace in the manner
of the *cento*, or patchwork. At about the same
time, the famous Hrosvitha of Gandersheim
writes her six Christian dramas patterned after
Terence, and in them uses Horace. Mention
by Walter of Speyer, and interest shown by
the active monastery on the Tegernsee, are
of the same period. The tenth century is sometimes spoken of as the Latin Renaissance under
the Ottos, the first of whom, called the Great,
crowned Emperor at Rome in 962, welcomed
scholars at his court and made every effort to
promote learning.

The momentum of intellectual interest is
not lost in the eleventh century. Paris becomes its most ardent center, with Reims,
Orléans, and Fleury also of note. The *Codex
Parisinus* belongs to this period. German
activity, too, is at its height, especially in the
education of boys for the church. Italy affords
one catalogue mention, of a Horace copied
under Desiderius. Peter Damian was its man
of greatest learning, but the times were intel-
lectually stagnant. The popes were occupied
by rivalry with the emperors. It was the century of Gregory the Seventh and Canossa.

In the twelfth century came the struggle of the Hohenstaufen with the Italian cities, and the disorder and turmoil of the rise of the communes and the division of Italy. One catalogue shows a Horace, and one manuscript dates from the time. England and France are united by the Norman Conquest in much the same way as Germany and France had been associated in the kingdom of Charlemagne. It is the century of Roger Bacon. Especially in Germany, England, and France, it is the age of the Crusades and the knightly orders. It is an age of the spread of culture among the common people. In France, it is the age of the monastery of Cluny, and the age of Abelard. Education and travel became the mode. In general, acquaintance with Horace among cultivated men may now be taken for granted. The *Epistles* and *Satires* find more favor than the *Odes*. Five hundred and twenty citations of the former and seventy-seven of the latter have been collected for the twelfth century.

The thirteenth century marks a decline in the intellectual life. The Crusades exhaust the energies of the time, and detract from its literary interest. The German rulers and the Italian ecclesiasts are absorbed in the struggle for supremacy between pope and emperor. Scholasticism overshadows humanism. The humanistic tradition of Charlemagne has died out, and the intellectual ideal is represented by Vincent of Beauvais and the *Speculum Historiale*. There is no mention of Horace in the catalogues of Italy. The manuscripts of France are careless, the comments and glosses poor. The decline will continue until arrested by the Renaissance.

It must not be forgotten that among all these scattered and flickering attentions to Horace there was the constant nucleus of instruction in the school. That he was used for this purpose first in the Carolingian cloister-schools, and later in the secular schools which grew to independent existence as a result of the vigorous spread of educational spirit, cannot be doubtful. Gerbert, dying at the beginning of the eleventh century as Pope Sylvester II, is known to have interpreted Horace in his school. This is the oldest direct evidence of the scholastic use of Horace, but other proofs are to be seen in the commentaries of the medieval period, all of which are of a kind suitable for school use, and in the marginal annotations, often in the native tongue.

The decline of humane studies in the thirteenth and fourteenth centuries meant also
the decline of interest in Horace, who had
always been above all the poet of the cultivated few. At the beginning of the thirteenth
century in Italy, nowhere but at Bologna and
Rome was Latin taught except as the elemen-
tary instruction necessary to the study of civil
and canonical law. Gaufried of Vinesaux,
coming from England to Italy, and composing
an *Ars Dictaminis* and a *Poietria Nova* containing Horatian reminiscences, is one of two
or three significant examples of Latin teachers
who concerned themselves with literature as
well as language. Coluccio Salutati, wanting
to buy a copy of Horace in 1370, is apparently
unable to find it. The decline of interest in
Horace will be arrested only by the Rebirth of
Learning.

The intellectual movement back to the classical authors and the classical civilizations is
well called the Rebirth. The brilliance of the
new era as compared with the thousand years
that lead to it from the most high and palmiest
days of Rome is such as to dim almost to darkness the brightest days of medieval culture.
The new life into which Horace is now to

enter will be so spirited and full that the old
life, though by no means devoid of active influence in society at large and in the individual
soul, will seem indeed like a long death and a
waiting for the resurrection into a new heaven
and a new earth.

4. HORACE AND MODERN TIMES

THE REBIRTH OF HORACE

THE national character of the *Aeneid* gave
Virgil a greater appeal than Horace in ancient
Roman times. In the Middle Age, his qualities
as story-teller and poet of the compassionate
heart, together with his fame as necromancer
and prophet, made still more pronounced the
favor in which he was held. The ignorance
of the earlier centuries of the period could not
appreciate Horace the logical, the intellectual,
the difficult, while the schematized religion and
knowledge of the later were not attracted by
Horace the philosophical and individual.

With the Renaissance and its quickening of
intellectual life in general, and in particular
the value it set upon personality and individ-
ualism, the positions of the poets were reversed. For four hundred years now it can

hardly be denied that Horace rather than Virgil has been the representative Latin poet of humanism.

This is not to say that Horace is greater than Virgil, or that he is as great. Virgil is still the poet of stately movement and golden narrative, the poet of the grand style. Owing to the greater facility with which he may be read, he is also still the poet of the young and of greater numbers. With the coming of the new era he did not lose in the esteem that is based upon the appreciation of literary art, but rather gained.

It will be better to say that Horace finally came more fully into his own. This was not because he changed. He did not change. The times changed. The barriers of intellectual sloth and artificiality fell away, and men became accessible to him. Virgil lost nothing of his old-time appeal to the fancy and to the ear, but Horace's virtues also were discovered: his distinction in word and phrase, his understanding of the human heart. Virgil lost nothing of his charm for youth and age, but Horace was discovered as the poet of the riper and more thoughtful mind. Virgil remained the admired, but Horace became the friend. Virgil remained the guide, but Horace became the companion. " Virgil," says Oliver Wendell Holmes, " has been the object of an adoration amounting almost to worship, but he will often be found on the shelf, while Horace lies on the student's table, next his hand."

The nature and extent of Horace's influence upon modern letters and life will be best brought into relief by a brief historical review. It is not necessary to this purpose, nor would it be possible, within ordinary limits, to enter into a detailed account. It will be appropriate to begin with Italy.

i. IN ITALY

Horace did not spring immediately into prominence with the coming of the Renaissance, whether elsewhere or in Italy. As might be expected, the essentially epic and medieval Dante found inspiration in Virgil rather than in Horace, though the *Ars Poetica* was known to him and quoted more than once as authority on style. " This is what our master Horace teaches," runs one of the passages, " when at the beginning of *Poetry* he says, ' Choose a

[106]

subject, etc.' " The imperfect idea of Horace formed in Dante's mind is indicated by the one verse in the *Divina Commedia* which refers to him:

L' altro è Orazio satiro che viene, —

The other coming is Horace the satirist.

With Petrarch, the first great figure to emerge from the obscure vistas of medievalism, the case was different. The first modern who really understood the classics understood Horace also, and did him greater justice than fell to his lot again for many generations. The copy of Horace's works which he acquired on November 28, 1347, remained by him until on the 18th of July in 1374 the venerable poet and scholar was found dead at the age of seventy among his books. Fond as he was of Virgil, Cicero, and Seneca, he had an intimate and affectionate knowledge of Horace, to whom there are references in all his works, and from whom he enriched his philosophy of life. Even his greatest and most original creation, the *Canzoniere*, is not without marks of Horace, and their fewness here, as well as their character, are a sign that Petrarch's familiarity was not of the artificial sort, but based on real assimilation of the poet. His letter to Horace begins:

> Salve o dei lirici modi sovrano,
> Salve o degl' Itali gloria ed onor, —

> *Hail! Sovereign of the lyric measure,*
> *Hail! Italy's great pride and treasure;*

and, after recounting the qualities of the poet, and acknowledging him as guide, teacher, and lord, concludes:

> Tanto è l' amor che a te m'avvince; tanto
> È degli affetti miei donno il tuo canto —

> *So great the love that bindeth me to thee;*
> *So ruleth in my heart thy minstrelsy.*

But Petrarch is a torch-bearer so far in advance of his successors that the illumination almost dies out again before they arrive. It was not until well into the fifteenth century that the long and numerous line of imitators, translators, adapters, parodists, commentators editors, and publishers began, which has continued to the present day. The modern-Latin poets in all countries were the first, but their efforts soon gave place to attempts in the vernacular tongues. The German Eduard

Stemplinger, in his *Life of the Horatian Lyric
Since the Renaissance,* published in 1906,
knows 90 English renderings of the entire *Odes*
of Horace, 70 German, 100 French, and 48
Italian. Some are in prose, some even in dia-
lect. The poet of Venusia is made a Bur-
gundian, a Berliner, and even a Platt-deutsch.
All of these are attempts to transfuse Horace
into the veins of modern life, and are significant of their authors' conviction as to the
vitalizing power of the ancient poet. No author from among the classics has been so frequently translated as Horace.

Petrarch, as we have seen, led the modern
world by a century in the appreciation of
Horace. It was in 1470, ninety-six years after
the laureate's death, that Italy achieved the
first printed edition of the poet, which was also
the first in the world. This was followed in
1474 by a printing of Acro's notes, grown by
accretion since their origin in the third century
into a much larger body of commentary. In
1476 was published the first Horace containing
both text and notes, which were those of Acro
and Porphyrio, and in 1482 appeared Landinus's notes, the first printed commentary on
Horace by a modern humanist. Landinus was

prefaced by a Latin poem of Politian's, who, with Lorenzo dei Medici, was a sort of arbiter in taste, and who produced in 1500 a Horace of his own. Mancinelli, who, like many other scholars of the time, gave public readings and interpretations of Horace and other classics, in 1492 dedicated to the celebrated enthusiast Pomponius Laetus an edition of the *Odes, Epodes,* and *Secular Hymn,* in which he so successfully integrated the comments of Acro, Porphyrio, Landinus, and himself, that for the next hundred years it remained the most authoritative Horace. In Italy, between 1470 and 1500, appeared no fewer than 44 editions of the poet, while in France there were four and in Germany about ten. Venice alone published, from 1490 to 1500, thirteen editions containing text and commentary by " The Great Four," as they were called. The famous Aldine editions began to appear in 1501. Besides Venice, Florence, and Rome, Ferrara came early to be a brilliant center of Horatian study, Lionel d'Este and the Guarini preparing the way for the more distinguished, if less scholastic, discipleship of Ariosto and Tasso. Naples and the South displayed little activity.

Roughly speaking, the later fifteenth century

was the age of manuscript recovery, commentary, and publication; the sixteenth, the century of translation, imitation, and ambitious attempt to rival the ancients on their own ground; the seventeenth and eighteenth, the centuries of critical erudition, with many commentaries and versions and much discussion of the theory of translation; and the nineteenth, the century of scientific revision and reconstruction. In the last movement, Italy had comparatively small part. Among her translators during these centuries must be mentioned Ludovico Dolce, whose excellent rendering of the *Satires* and *Epistles* was a product of the early sixteenth; Scipione Ponsa, whose faithful *Ars Poetica* in *ottava rima* appeared in the first half of the seventeenth; the advocate Borgianelli, whose brilliant version of Horace entire belongs to the second half; and the Venetian Abriani, whose complete *Odes* in the original meters, the first achievement of the kind, was a not unsuccessful performance which has taken its place among Horatian curiosities. Among literary critics are the names of Gravina, whose *Della Ragione Poetica*, full of sound scholarship and refreshing good sense, appeared in 1716 at Naples; Volpi of Padua, author of a treatise on

Satire, in which the merits of Lucilius, Horace, Juvenal, and Persius were effectively discussed; and their followers, Algarotti the Venetian and Vannetti of Roveredo, in whom Horatian criticism reached its greatest altitude.

If we look outside the field of scholastic endeavor and academic imitation, and attempt to discern the effect of Horace in actual literary creation, we are confronted by the difficulty of determining exactly where imitation and adaptation cease to be artificial, and reach the degree of individuality and independence which entitles them to the name of originality. If we are to include here such authors as are manifestly indebted to suggestion or inspiration from Horace, and yet are quite as manifestly modern and Italian, we may note at least the names of Petrarch, already mentioned; the famous Cardinal Bembo, whose ideal, to write "thoughtfully and little," was a reflection of Horace; Ariosto, whose satires are in the Horatian spirit, and who, complaining to his brother Alessandro of the attitude of his patron, Cardinal Hippolyto d'Este, recites the story of the fox and the weasel, changing them to donkey and rat; Chiabrera of Savona, who wrote satire honeycombed with Horatian allusion and permeated by Horatian spirit, and who, in Leopardi's opinion, had he lived in a different age, would have been a second Horace; Testi of Ferrara, whom Ariosto's enthusiasm for Horace so kindled that he gravitated from the modern spirit to the classical; Parini of Milan, whose poem, *Alla Musa,* is Horatian in spirit and phrase; Leopardi, who composed a parody on the *Ars Poetica;* Prati, who transmuted *Epode II* into the *Song of Hygieia;* and Carducci, whose use of Horatian meters, somewhat strained, is due to the conscious desire of making Italy's past greatness serve the present. The names of Bernardo Tasso and Torquato Tasso might be added.

It is not impossible, also, that the musical debt of the world to Italy is in a measure owing to Horace. Whether the music which accompanied the *Odes* as they emerged from the Middle Age was only the invention of monks, or the survival of actual Horatian music from antiquity, is a question hardly to be answered; but the setting of Horace to music in the Renaissance was not without an influence. In 1507, Tritonius composed four-voice parts for twenty-two different meters of Horace and other poets. In 1526, Michael engaged in the same effort, and in 1534 Senfl developed the youthful compositions of Tritonius. All this was for school purposes. With the beginnings of Italian opera, these compositions, in which the music was without measure and held strictly to the service of poetry, came to an end. It is not unreasonable to suspect that in these early attempts at the union of ancient verse and music there exist the beginnings of the musical drama.

ii. IN FRANCE

France, where the great majority of Horatian manuscripts were preserved, was the first to produce a translation of the *Odes*. Grandichan in 1541, and Pelletier in 1545, published translations of the *Ars Poetica* which had important consequences. The famous Pleiad, whose most brilliant star, Pierre de Ronsard, was king of poetry for more than a score of years, were enthusiastic believers in the imitation of the classics as a means for the improvement of letters in France. Du Bellay, the second in magnitude, published in 1550 his *Deffence et illustration de la langue françoyse,* a manifesto of the Pleiad full of quotations from the *Ars*

Poetica refuting a similar work of Sibilet published in 1548. Ronsard himself is said to have been the first to use the word " ode " for Horace's lyrics. The meeting of the two, in 1547, is regarded as the beginning of the French school of Renaissance poetry. Horace thus became at the beginning an influence of the first magnitude in the actual life of modern French letters. In 1579 appeared Mondot's complete translation. The versions of Dacier and Sanadon, in prose, in the earlier eighteenth century, were an innovation provoking spirited opposition in Italy. The line of translators, imitators, and enthusiasts in France is as numerous as that of other countries. The list of great authors inspired by Horace includes such names as Montaigne, " The French Horace," Malherbe, Regnier, Boileau, La Fontaine, Corneille, Racine, Molière, Voltaire, Jean Baptiste Rousseau, Le Brun, André Chénier, De Musset.

iii. IN GERMANY

In Germany, the Renaissance movement had its pronounced beginning at Heidelberg. In that city began also the active study of Horace, in the lectures on Horace in 1456. The *Epistles* were first printed in 1482 at Leipzig, the *Epodes* in 1488, and in 1492 appeared the first complete Horace. Up to 1500, about ten editions had been published, only those of 1492 and 1498 being Horace entire, and none of them with commentary except that of 1498, which had a few notes and metrical signs to indicate the structure of the verse. The first German to translate a poem of Horace was Johann Fischart, 1550–90, who rendered the second *Epode* in 145 rhymed couplets. The famous Silesian, Opitz, " father of German poetry," and his followers, were to Germany what the Pleiad were to France. His work on poetry, 1624, was grounded in Horace, and was long the canon. Bucholz, in 1639, produced the first translation of an entire book of the *Odes* in German. Weckherlin, 1548–1653, translated three *Odes*, Gottsched of Leipzig, 1700–66, and Breitinge of Zurich, confess Horace as master of the art of poetry, and their cities become the centers of many translations. Günther, 1695–1728, the most gifted lyric poet of his race before Klopstock, made Horace his companion and confidant of leisure hours. Hagedorn, 1708–54, forms his philosophy from

Horace, — " my friend, my teacher, my companion." Of Ramler, for thirty-five years dictator of the Berlin literary world, who translated and published some of the *Odes* in 1769 and was called the German Horace, Lessing said that no sovereign had ever been so beautifully addressed as was Frederick the Great in his imitation of the Maecenas ode. The epochmaking Klopstock, 1724–1803, quotes, translates, and imitates Horace, and uses Horatian subjects. Heinse reads him and writes of him enthusiastically, and Platen, 1796–1835, is so full of Homer and Horace that he can do nothing of his own. Lessing and Herder are devoted Horatians, though Herder thinks that Lessing and Winckelmann are too unreserved in their enthusiasm for the imitation of classical letters. Goethe praises Horace for lyric charm and for understanding of art and life, and studies his meters while composing the *Elegies*. Nietzsche's letters abound in quotation and phrase. Even the Church in Germany shows the impress of Horace in some of her greatest hymns, which are in Alcaics and Sapphics of Horatian origin. To speak of the German editors, commentators, and critics of the nineteenth century would be almost to re-

view the history of Horace in modern school
and university; such has been the ardor of the
German soul and the industry of the German
mind.

iv. IN SPAIN

A glance at the use of Horace in Spain will
afford not the least edifying of modern examples. The inventories of Spanish libraries in
the Middle Age rarely contain the name of
Horace, or the names of his lyric brethren,
Catullus, Tibullus, and Propertius. Virgil,
Lucan, Martial, Seneca, and Pliny are much
more frequent. It was not until the fifteenth
century that reminiscences of the style and
ideas of Horace began to appear in quantity.
Imitation rather than translation was the
vehicle of Spanish enthusiasm. The fountain
of Horatianism in Spain was the imitation of
Epode II, Beatus Ille, by the Marquis de San-
tillana, one of Castile's two first sonneteers, in
the first half of the fifteenth century. Gar-
cilaso also produced many imitations of the
Odes. The Horatian lyric seemed especially
congenial to the Spanish spirit and language.
Fray Luís de León, of Salamanca, the first
real Spanish poet, and the most inspired of all

the Spanish lovers of Horace, was an example of the poet translating the poet where both were great men. He not only brought back to life once more "that marvelous sobriety, that rapidity of idea and conciseness of phrase, that terseness and brilliance, that sovereign calm and serenity in the spirit of the artist," which characterized the ancient poet, but added to the Horatian lyre the new string of Christian mysticism, and thus wedded the ancient and the modern. "Luís de León is our great Horatian poet," says Menéndez y Pelayo. Lope de Vega wrote an *Ode to Liberty,* and was influenced by the *Epistles.* The *Flores de Poetas ilustres de España,* arranged by Pedro Espinosa and published in 1605 at Valladolid, included translations of eighteen odes. Hardly a lyric poet of the eighteenth century failed to turn some part of Horace into Spanish. Salamanca perfected the ode, Seville the epistle, Aragon the satire. Mendoza in his nine *Epistles* shows his debt to Horace. In 1592, Luís de Zapata published at Lisbon a not very successful verse translation of the *Ars Poetica.* In 1616, Francisco de Cascales of Murcia published *Fablas Poeticas,* containing in dialogue the substance of the same composition, which had been translated by Espinel, 1551–1624, and which was translated again in 1684, twice in 1777, and in 1827. Seville founded a Horatian Academy. The greatest of the Spanish translators of Horace entire was Javier de Burgos, whose edition of four volumes, 1819–1844, is called by Menéndez y Pelayo the only readable complete translation of Horace, " one of the most precious and enviable jewels of our modern literature," and " perhaps the best of all Horaces in the neo-Latin tongues." The nearest rival of Burgos was Martinez de la Rosa. The greatest Spanish scholar and critic of Horace is Menéndez y Pelayo, editor of the *Odes*, 1882, and author of *Horacio en España*, 1885.

In the index of *Horacio en España* are to be found the names of 165 Castilian translators of the poet, 50 Portuguese, 10 Catalan, 2 Asturian, and 1 Galician. There appear the names of 29 commentators. Of complete translations, there are 6 Castilian and 1 Portuguese; of complete translations of the *Odes*, 6 Castilian and 7 Portuguese; of the *Satires*, 1 Castilian and 2 Portuguese; of the *Epistles*, 1 Castilian and 1 Portuguese; of the *Ars Poetica*, 35 Castilian, 11 Portuguese, and 1

Catalan. The sixteenth century translators were distinguished in general by facility and grace, the freshness and abandon of youth, and a considerable degree of freedom, or even license. Those of the eighteenth show a gain in accuracy and a loss in spirit.

v. IN ENGLAND

The appeal of Horace in England and English-speaking countries has been as fruitful as elsewhere in scholarship, with the possible exception of Germany. In its effect upon the actual fibre of literature and life, it has been more fruitful.

A review of Horatian study in England would include the names of Talbot and Baxter, but, above all, of the incomparably brilliant Richard Bentley, despite his excesses, themselves due to his very genius, the most famous and most stimulating critic and commentator of Horace the world has seen. His edition, appearing in 1711, provoked in 1717 the anti-Bentleian rejoinder of Richard Johnson, and in 1721 the more ambitious but equally unsuccessful attempt to discredit him by the Scotch Alexander Cunningham. The primacy in the study of

Horace which Bentley conferred upon England had been enjoyed previously by the Low Countries and France, to which it had passed from Italy in the second half of the sixteenth century. The immediate sign of this transfer of the center to northern lands was the publication in 1561 at Lyons of the edition containing the text revision and critical notes of Lambinus and the commentary of the famous Cruquius of Bruges. The celebrated Scaliger was unfavorably disposed to Horace, who found a defender in Heinsius, another scholar of the Netherlands. D'Alembert, who became a sort of *Ars Poetica* to translators, published his *Observations* at Amsterdam in 1763.

An account of the English translations of the poet would include many renderings of individual poems, such as those of Dryden, Sir Stephen E. De Vere, and John Conington, and the version of Theodore Martin, probably the most successful complete metrical translation of Horace in any language. It is literally true that " every theory of translation has been exemplified in some English rendering of Horace."

It is in the field of literature, however, that the manifestations of Horace's hold upon the

English are most numerous and most significant. Even Shakespeare's "small Latin" includes him, in *Titus Andronicus*:

Demetrius.

What's here? A scroll, and written round about!
Let's see:

> Integer vitae scelerisque purus
> Non eget Mauri jaculis nec arcu.

Chiron.

> *O, 'tis a verse in Horace; I know it well:*
> *I read it in the grammar long ago.*

The mere mention of English authors in
poetry and prose who were touched and kindled
by the Horatian flame would amount to a review of the whole course of English literature.
It would begin principally with Spenser and
Ben Jonson, who in some measure represented
in their land what the Pleiad meant in France,
and Opitz and his following in Germany.
"Steep yourselves in the classics," was Jonson's counsel, and his countrymen did thus
steep themselves to such a degree that it is
possible for the student to say of Milton's
times: "The door to English literature and

history of the seventeenth century is open wide
to those who are at ease in the presence of
Latin. Many writings and events of the time
may doubtless be understood and enjoyed by
readers ignorant of the classics, but to them
the heart and spirit of the period as a whole
will hardly be revealed. Poetry, philosophy,
history, biography, controversy, sermons, cor-
respondence, even conversation, — all have
come down to us from the age of Milton either
written in or so touched with Latin that one is
compelled to enter seventeenth century England by way of Rome as Rome must be entered
by way of Athens."

Great as was the vogue of Latin in the earlier
centuries, it was the first half of the eighteenth,
the most critical period in English letters, that
realized to the full the virtues of Horace. His
words in the *Ars Poetica* " were accepted, even
more widely than the laws of Aristotle, as the
standard of critical judgment. Addison and
Steele by their choice of mottoes for their
periodicals, Prior by his adoption of a type
of lyric that has since his time been designated
as Horatian, and Pope with his imposing series
of *Imitations*, gave such an impulse to the
already widespread interest that it was carried

on through the whole of the century." " Horace
may be said to pervade the literature of the
eighteenth century in three ways: as a teacher
of political and social morality; as a master of
the art of poetry; and as a sort of *elegantiae
arbiter*." Richardson, Sterne, Smollett, and
Fielding, Gay, Samuel Johnson, Chesterfield,
and Walpole, were all familiar with and fond
of Horace, and took him unto themselves.

In the nineteenth century, Wordsworth has
an intimate familiarity with Virgil, Catullus,
and Horace, but loves Horace best; Coleridge
thinks highly of his literary criticism; Byron,
who never was greatly fond of him, frequently
quotes him; Shelley reads him with pleasure;
Browning's *The Ring and the Book* contains
many quotations from him; Thackeray makes
use of phrases from the *Odes* " with an ease
and facility which nothing but close intimacy
could produce "; Andrew Lang addresses to
him the most charming of his *Letters to Dead
Authors;* and Austin Dobson is inspired by
him in many of his exquisite poems in lighter
vein. These names, and those in the para-
graphs preceding, are not all that might be
mentioned. The literature of England is honeycombed with the classic authors in general,

and Horace is among the foremost. Without him and without the classics, a great part of our literary patrimony is of little use.

vi. IN THE SCHOOLS

Of the place of Horace in the schools and universities of all these countries, and of the world of western civilization in general, it is hardly necessary to speak. The enlightened sentiment of the five hundred years since the death of Petrarch has been enthusiastic in the conviction that the Greek and Latin classics are indispensable to instruction of the first quality, and that among them Horace is of exceeding value as a model of poetic taste and as an influence in the formation of a philosophy of life. If his place has been less secure in latter days, it is due less to alteration of that conviction than to extension of the educational system to the utilitarian arts and sciences, and to the passing of educational control from the few to the general average.

III. HORACE THE DYNAMIC

THE CULTIVATED FEW

W E HAVE followed in such manner and at such length as is possible for our purpose the fortunes of Horace through the ages from his death and the death of the Empire in whose service his pen was employed to our own times. We have seen that he never was really forgotten, and that there never was a time of long duration when he ceased to be of real importance to some portion of mankind.

The recital of historical fact is at best a narration of circumstance to which there clings little of the warmth of life. An historical event itself is but the cumulated and often frigid result of intimate original forces that may have meant long travail of body and soul before the act of realization became possible. The record of the event in chronicle or its commemoration in monument is only the sign that at some time there occurred a significant moment rendered inevitable by previous stirrings of life whose intensity, if not whose very identity, are forgotten or no longer realized.

Thus the enumeration of manuscript revisions, translations, imitations, and scholastic editions of Horace may also seem at first sight the narrative of cold detail. There may be readers who, remembering the scant stream of the cultivated few who tided the poet through the centuries of darkness, and the comparative rareness of cultivated men at all times, will be slow to be convinced of any real impress of Horace upon the life of men. They especially who reflect that during all the long sweep of time the majority of those who have known him, and even of those who have been stirred to enthusiasm by him, have known him through the compulsion of the school, and who reflect farther on the artificialities, the insincerities, the pettinesses, the abuses, and the hatreds of the class-room, the joy with which at the end the text-book is dropped or bidden an even more violent farewell, and the apparently total oblivion that follows, will be inclined to view as exaggeration the most moderate estimate of our debt to him.

Yet skepticism would be without warrant.

The presence of any subject in an educational scheme represents the sincere, and often the fervent, conviction that it is worthy of the place. In the case of literary subjects, the nearer the approach to pure letters, the less demonstrable the connection between instruction and the winning of livelihood, the more intense the conviction. The immortality of literature and the arts, which surely has been demonstrated by time, the respect in which they are held by a world so intent on mere living that of its own motion it would never heed, is the work of the passionate few whose enthusiasms and protestations never allow the common crowd completely to forget, and keep forever alive in it the uneasy sense of imperfection. That Horace was preserved for hundreds of years by monastery and school, that the fact of acquaintance with him is due to his place in modern systems of education, are not mere statements empty of life. They represent the noble enthusiasms of enlightened men. The history of human progress has been the history of enthusiasms. Without enthusiasms, the fabric of civilization would collapse in a day into the chaos of barbarism.

To give greater completeness and reality to

our account of Horace's place among men,
ancient and modern, we must in some way
add to the narrative of formal fact the demonstration of his influence in actual operation.
In the case of periods obscure and remote, this
is hardly possible. In the case of modern
times it is not so difficult. For the recent
centuries, as proof of the peculiar power of
Horace, we have the abundant testimony of
literature and biography.

Let us call this influence the Dynamic Power
of Horace. Dynamic power is the power that
explodes men, so to speak, into physical or
spiritual action, that operates by inspiration,
expansion, fertilization, vitalization, and results in the living of a fuller life. If we can
be shown concrete instances of Horace enriching the lives of men by increasing their
love and mastery of art or multiplying their
means of happiness, we shall not only appreciate better the poet's meaning for the present
day, but be better able to imagine his effect
upon men in the remoter ages whose life is less
open to scrutiny.

Our purpose will best be accomplished by
demonstrating the very specific and pronounced
effect of Horace, first, upon the formation of

the literary ideal; second, upon the actual creation of literature; and, third, upon living itself.

1. Horace and the Literary Ideal

There is no better example of the direct effect of Horace than the part played in the discipline of letters by the *Ars Poetica*. This work is a literary *causerie* inspired in part by the reading of Alexandrian criticism, but in larger part by experience. In it the author's uppermost themes, as in characteristic manner he allows himself to be led on from one thought to another, are unity, consistency, propriety, truthfulness, sanity, and carefulness. Such has been its power by reason of inner substance and outward circumstance that it has been at times exalted into a court of appeal hardly less authoritative than Aristotle himself, from whom in large part it ultimately derives.

We have seen how the Pleiad, with Du Bellay and Ronsard leading, seized upon the classics as a means of elevating the literature of France, and how the treatise of Du Bellay which was put forth as their manifesto was full of matter from the *Ars Poetica*, which two

years previously has served Sibilet also, whose
work Du Bellay attacked. A century later,
Boileau's *L'Art Poétique* testifies again to the
inspiration of Horace, who is made the means
of riveting still more firmly upon French
drama, for good or ill, the strict rules that have
always governed it; and by the time of Boileau's
death the program of the Pleiad is revived a
second time by Jean Baptiste Rousseau. Opitz
and Gottsched in the seventeenth and eighteenth centuries are for Germany what Du
Bellay and Boileau were for France in the
sixteenth and seventeenth. Literary Spain of
the latter fifteenth and early sixteenth centuries was under the same influence. The
Spanish peninsula, according to Menéndez y
Pelayo, has produced no fewer than forty-seven
translations of the *Ars Poetica*. Even in England, always less tractable in the matter of
rules than the Latin countries, Ben Jonson and
his friends are in some sort another Pleiad,
and the treatise possesses immense authority
throughout the centuries. We turn the pages
of Cowl's *The Theory of Poetry in England*,
a book of critical extracts illustrating the development of poetry " in doctrines and ideas
from the sixteenth century to the nineteenth

century," and note Ben Jonson and Wordsworth referring to or quoting Horace in the section on Poetic Creation; Dryden and Temple appealing to him and Aristotle on the Rules; Hurd quoting him on Nature and the Stage; Roger Ascham, Ben Jonson, and Dryden citing him as an example on Imitation; Dryden and Chapman calling him master and law-giver on Translation; Samuel Johnson referring to him on the same subject; and Ben Jonson and Dryden using him on Functions and Principles of Criticism. " Horace," writes Jonson, " an author of much civility, . . . an excellent and true judge upon cause and reason, not because he thought so, but because he knew so out of use and experience." Pope, in the *Essay on Criticism*, describes with peculiar felicity both Horace's critical manner and the character of the authority, persuasive rather than tyrannical, which he exercises over Englishmen:

" *Horace still charms with graceful negligence,*
  And without method talks us into sense;
  Will, like a friend, familiarly convey
  The truest notions in the easiest way."

But the dynamic power of the *Ars Poetica* will be still better appreciated if we assemble some of its familiar principles. Who has not heard of and wondered at the hold the "Rules" have had upon modern drama, especially in France, — the rule of five acts, no more and no less; the rule of three actors only, liberalized into the rule of economy; the rule of the unities in time, place, and action; the rule against the mingling of the tragic and comic "kinds"; the rule against the artificial dénouement? Who has not heard of French playwrights composing "with one eye on the clock" for fear of violating the unity of time, or of their delight in the writing of drama as in "a difficult game well played?" If Alexandrian criticism, and, back of it, Aristotle, were ultimately responsible for the rules, Horace was their disseminator in later times, and was looked up to as final authority. Who has not heard and read repeatedly the now commonplace injunctions to be appropriate and consistent in character-drawing; to avoid, on the one hand, clearness at the cost of diffuseness, and, on the other, brevity at the cost of obscurity; to choose subject-matter suited to one's powers; to respect the authority of the master-

piece and to con by night and by day the great
Greek exemplars; to feel the emotion one wishes
to rouse; to stamp the universal with the mark
of individual genius; to be straightforward and
rapid and omit the unessential; to be truthful
to life; to keep the improbable and the horrible
behind the scenes; to be appropriate in meter
and diction; to keep clear of the fallacy of
poetic madness; to look for the real sources of
successful writing in sanity, depth of knowledge, and experience with men; to remember
the mutual indispensability of genius and cultivation; to combine the pleasant and the useful; to deny one's self the indulgence of medi-
ocrity; never to compose unless under inspiration; to give heed to solid critical counsel;
to lock up one's manuscript for nine years
before giving it to the world; to destroy what
does not measure up to the ideal; to take ever-
lasting pains; to beware of the compliments of
good-natured friends? Not less familiar are
the apt figurative illustrations of the woman
beautiful above and an ugly fish below, the
purple patch, the painter who would forever
put in his cypress tree, the amphora that came
out a pitcher, the dolphin in the wood and the
boar in the waters, the sesquipedalian word,

[135]

the mountains in travail and the birth of the ridiculous mouse, the plunge *in medias res,* the praiser of the good old times, the exclusion of sane poets from Helicon, the counsellor who himself can write nothing, but will serve as whetstone for genius, the nodding of Homer.

Nor did the effects of this diffusion of Horatian precept consist merely in restraint upon the youthful and the impulsive, or confine themselves to the drama, with which the *Ars Poetica* was mainly concerned. The persuasive and authoritative counsels of the Roman poet have entered, so to speak, into the circulatory system of literary effort and become part of the lifeblood of modern enlightenment. Their great effect has been formative: the cultivation of character in literature.

2. Horace and Literary Creation

i. the translator's ideal

Besides the invisible, and the greatest, effect of Horace in the moulding of character in literature, is the visible effect in literary creation. His inspiration wrought by performance as well as by precept. The numerous

essays in verse and prose on the art of letters
which have been prompted by the *Ars Poetica*
are themselves examples of this effect. They
are not alone, however, though perhaps the
most apparent. The purer literature of the
lyric also inspired to creation, with results that
are far more charming, if less substantial.

In the case of the lyric inspired by the *Odes*,
as well as in the case of the critical essay inspired by the *Ars Poetica*, it is not always easy
to distinguish adaptation or imitation from actual creation. Bernardo Tasso's *Ode*, for example, and Giovanni Prati's *Song of Hygieia*,
while really independent poems, are so charged
with Horatian matter and spirit that one hesi-
tates to call them original. The same is true
of the many inspirations traceable to the famous *Beatus Ille Epode*, which, with such *Odes*
as *The Bandusian Spring, Pyrrha, Phidyle*, and
Chloe, have captured the fancy of modern
poets. Pope's *Solitude*, on the other hand,
while surely an inspiration of the second *Epode*,
shows hardly a mark affording proof of the fact.

To some of the most manifest imitations and
adaptations, it is impossible to deny originality.
The *Fifth Book of Horace*, by Kipling and
Graves, is an example. Thackeray's delightful

Ad Ministram is another example which must be classed as adaptation, yet such is its spontaneity that not to see in it an inspiration would be stupid and unjust:

AD MINISTRAM

Dear Lucy, you know what my wish is —
  I hate all your Frenchified fuss:
Your silly entrées and made dishes
  Were never intended for us.
No footman in lace and in ruffles
  Need dangle behind my arm-chair;
And never mind seeking for truffles
  Although they be ever so rare.

But a plain leg of mutton, my Lucy,
  I prithee get ready at three:
Have it smoking, and tender, and juicy,
  And what better meat can there be?
And when it has feasted the master,
  'Twill amply suffice for the maid;
Meanwhile I will smoke my canaster,
  And tipple my ale in the shade.

In similar strain of exquisite humor are the adaptations of the Whichers, American examples of spirit and skill not second to that of Thackeray:

MY SABINE FARM

LAUDABUNT ALII

Some people talk about " Noo Yo'k ";
  Of Cleveland many ne'er have done;
They sing galore of Baltimore,
  Chicago, Pittsburgh, Washington.

Others unasked their wit have tasked
  To sound unending praise of Boston —
Of bean-vines found for miles around
  And crooked streets that I get lost on.

Give me no jar of truck or car,
  No city smoke and noise of mills;
Rather the slow Connecticut's flow
  And sunny orchards on the hills.

There like the haze of summer days
  Before the wind flee care and sorrow.
In sure content each day is spent,
  Unheeding what may come to-morrow.

VITAS HINNULEO

DONE BY MR. WILLIAM WORDSWORTH

I met a little Roman maid;
She was just sixteen (she said),
And O! but she was sore afraid,
And hung her modest head.

A little fawn, you would have vowed,
That sought her mother's side,
And wandered lonely as a cloud
Upon the mountain wide.

Whene'er the little lizards stirred
She started in her fear;
In every rustling bush she heard
Some awful monster near.

" I'm not a lion; fear not so;
Seek not your timid dam." —
But Chloe was afraid, and O!
She knows not what I am:

A creature quite too bright and good
To be so much misunderstood.

Again, in Austin Dobson's exquisite *Triolet*, whether the inspiration of the poem itself is in Horace, or the inspiration, so far as Horace is concerned, lies in the choice of title after the verses were written, we must in either case confess a debt of great delight to the author of the *Ars Poetica:*

URCEUS EXIT

I *intended an Ode,*
   And it turned to a Sonnet.
I*t began* à la mode,
I *intended an Ode;*
B*ut Rose crossed the road*
   I*n her latest new bonnet;*
I *intended an Ode,*
   And it turned to a Sonnet.

The same observation applies equally to the same author's *Iocosa Lyra:*

IOCOSA LYRA

I*n our hearts is the great one of Avon*
        Engraven,
A*nd we climb the cold summits once built on*
        By Milton;

[141]

But at times not the air that is rarest
                    Is fairest,
And we long in the valley to follow
                    Apollo.

Then we drop from the heights atmospheric
                    To Herrick,
Or we pour the Greek honey, grown blander,
                    Of Landor,

Or our cosiest nook in the shade is
                    Where Praed is,
Or we toss the light bells of the mocker
                    With Locker.

O the song where not one of the Graces
                    Tightlaces, —
Where we woo the sweet Muses not starchly,
                    But archly, —

Where the verse, like a piper a-Maying
                    Comes playing, —
And the rhyme is as gay as a dancer
                    In answer,—

It will last till men weary of pleasure
                    In measure!
It will last till men weary of laughter . . .
                    And after!

Whatever we may say of the indebtedness of things like these to the letter of the ancient poet, we must acknowledge them all alike as examples of the dynamic power of Horace.

ii. CREATION

But there are other examples whose character as literary creation is still farther beyond question. Such a one, to mention one brilliant specimen in prose, is the letter of Andrew Lang to Horace. In verse, Austin Dobson again affords one of the happiest examples:

TO Q. H. F.

" *Horatius Flaccus*, B.C. 8,"
 There's not a doubt about the date, —
   You're dead and buried:
As you observed, the seasons roll;
And 'cross the Styx full many a soul
   Has Charon ferried,
Since, mourned of men and Muses nine,
They laid you on the Esquiline.

And that was centuries ago!
You'd think we'd learned enough, I know,
   To help refine us,

HORACE AND HIS INFLUENCE

Since last you trod the Sacred Street,
And tacked from mortal fear to meet
  The bore Crispinus;
Or, by your cold Digentia, set
The web of winter birding-net.

Ours is so far-advanced an age!
Sensation tales, a classic stage,
  Commodious villas!
We boast high art, an Albert Hall,
Australian meats, and men who call
  Their sires gorillas!
We have a thousand things, you see,
Not dreamt in your philosophy.

And yet, how strange! Our " world," today,
Tried in the scale, would scarce outweigh
  Your Roman cronies;
Walk in the Park, — you'll seldom fail
To find a Sybaris on the rail
  By Lydia's ponies,
Or hap on Barrus, wigged and stayed,
Ogling some unsuspecting maid.

The great Gargilius, then, behold!
His " long-bow " hunting tales of old
  Are now but duller;

Fair Neobule too! Is not
One Hebrus here, — from Aldershot?
        Aha, you colour!
Be wise. There old Canidia sits;
No doubt she's tearing you to bits.

And look, dyspeptic, brave, and kind,
Comes dear Maecenas, half behind
        Terentia's skirting;
Here's Pyrrha, " golden-haired " at will;
Prig Damasippus, preaching still;
        Asterie flirting, —
Radiant, of course. We'll make her black, —
Ask her when Gyges' ship comes back.

So with the rest. Who will may trace
Behind the new each elder face
        Defined as clearly;
Science proceeds, and man stands still;
Our " world " today's as good or ill, —
        As cultured (nearly),
As yours was, Horace! You alone,
Unmatched, unmet, we have not known.

But it is not only to comparatively independent creation that we must look. The dynamic
power of Horace is to be found at work even in
the translation of the poet. The fact that he has

had more translators than any other poet, ancient or modern, is itself an evidence of inspirational quality, but a greater proof lies in the variety and character of his translators and the quality of their achievement. A list of those who have felt in this way the stirrings of the Horatian spirit would include the names not only of many great men of letters, but of many great men of affairs, whose successes are to be counted among examples of genuine inspiration. Translation at its best is not mere craftsmanship, but creation, — in Roscommon's lines,

> 'Tis true, composing is the Nobler Part,
> But good Translation is no easy Art.

Theodore Martin's rendering of I. 21, *To a Jar of Wine*, already quoted in part, is an example. Another brilliant success is Sir Stephen E. De Vere's I. 31, *Prayer to Apollo*, quoted in connection with the poet's religious attitude. No less felicitous are Conington's spirited twelve lines, reproducing III. 26, *Vixi puellis*:

VIXI PUELLIS NUPER IDONEUS

For ladies' love I late was fit,
  And good success my warfare blest;
But now my arms, my lyre I quit,
  And hang them up to rust or rest.
Here, where arising from the sea
  Stands Venus, lay the load at last,
Links, crowbars, and artillery,
  Threatening all doors that dared be fast.
O Goddess! Cyprus owns thy sway,
  And Memphis, far from Thracian snow:
Raise high thy lash, and deal me, pray,
  That haughty Chloe just one blow!

To translate in this manner is beyond all doubt
to deserve the name of poet.

We may go still farther and claim for Horace
that he has been a dynamic power in the art of
translation, not only as it concerned his own
poems, but in its concern of translation as a
universal art. No other poet presents such
difficulties; no other poet has left behind him
so long a train of disappointed aspirants.
"Horace remains forever the type of the un-
translatable," says Frederic Harrison. Milton
attempts the *Pyrrha* ode in unrhymed meter,
and the light and bantering spirit of Horace

[147]

disappears. Milton is correct, polished, re-strained, and pure, but heavy and cold. An exquisite *jeu d'esprit* has been crushed to death:

What slender youth, bedew'd with liquid odours,
Courts thee on roses in some pleasant cave,
  Pyrrha? For whom bind'st thou
  In wreaths thy golden hair,
Plain in thy neatness? O how oft shall he
On faith and changèd gods complain, and seas
  Rough with black winds and storms
  Unwonted shall admire!
Who now enjoys thee credulous, all gold,
Who, always vacant, always amiable
  Hopes thee, of flattering gales
  Unmindful! Hapless they
To whom thou untried seem'st fair! Me in my
  vowed
Picture, the sacred wall declares to have hung
  My dank and dropping weeds
  To the stern God of Sea.

But let the attempt be made to avoid the ponderous movement and excessive sobriety of Milton, and to communicate the Horatian airi-ness, and there is a loss in conciseness and reserve:

What scented youth now pays you court,
  Pyrrha, in shady rose-strewn spot
Dallying in love's sweet sport?
  For whom that innocent-seeming knot
In which your golden strands you dress
With all the art of artlessness?

Deluded lad! How oft he'll weep
  O'er changèd gods! How oft, when dark
The billows roughen on the deep,
  Storm-tossed he'll see his wretched bark!
Unused to Cupid's quick mutations,
In store for him what tribulations!

But now his joy is all in you;
  He thinks your heart is purest gold;
Expects you'll always be love-true,
  And never, never, will grow cold.
Poor mariner on summer seas,
Untaught to fear the treacherous breeze!

Ah, wretched whom your Siren call
  Deludes and brings to watery woes!
For me — yon plaque on Neptune's wall
  Shows I've endured the seaman's throes.
My drenchèd garments hang there, too:
Henceforth I shun the enticing blue.

It is not improbable that the struggle of the centuries with the difficulties of rendering Horace has been a chief influence in the development of our present exacting ideal of translation; so exacting indeed that it has defeated its purpose. By emphasis upon the impossibility of rendering accurately the content of poetry in the form of poetry, scholastic discussion of the theory of translation has led first to despair, and next from despair to the scientific and unaesthetic principle of rendering into exact prose all forms of literature alike. The twentieth century has thus opened again and settled in opposite manner the old dispute of the French D'Alembert and the Italian Salvini in the seventeen-hundreds, which was resolved by actual results in favor of D'Alembert and fidelity to spirit as opposed to Salvini and fidelity to letter.

In what we have said thus far of the dynamic power of Horace in literary creation, we have dealt with visible results. We should not be misled, however, by the satisfaction of seeing plainly in imitation, adaptation, translation, quotation, or real creation, the mark of Horatian influence. The discipline of the literary ideal in the individual, and the moulding of character in literature as an organism, are effects less clearly visible, but, after all, of greater value. If the bread and meat of human sustenance should appear in the body as recognizable bread and meat, it would hardly be a sign of health. Its value is in the strength conferred by assimilation. With all respect and gratitude for creation manifestly due to Horace, we must also realize that this is but a superficial result as compared with the chastening restraint of expression and the health and vigor of content that have been encouraged by allegiance to him, but are known by no special marks. It is no bad sign when we turn the pages of the *Oxford Selections of Verse* in the various modern languages and find but few examples of the visible sort of Horatian influence. To detect the more invisible sort requires the keen eye and the sensitive spirit of the poet-scholar, but the reader not so specially qualified may have faith that it exists. With Goethe writing of Horace as a " great, glowing, noble poet, full of heart, who with the power of his song sweeps us along, lifts us, and inspires us," with Menéndez y Pelayo in Spain defining the Horatian lyric, whether Christian or pagan, by " sobriety of thought, rhythmic lightness, the absence of artificial adornment, unlimited care in execution, and brevity," and holding this ideal aloft as the influence needed by the modern lyric, and with no countries or periods without leaders in poetry and criticism uttering similar sentiments and exhortations, it would be difficult not to believe in a substantial Horatian effect on literary culture, however slight the external marks.

3. HORACE IN THE LIVING OF MEN

LET us take leave of these illustrations of the dynamic power of Horace in letters, and consider in conclusion his power as shown directly in the living of men.

First of all, we may include in the dynamic working of the poet his stirring of the heart by pure delight. If this is not the highest and the ultimate effect of poetry, it is after all the first and the essential effect. Without the giving of pleasure, no art becomes really the possession of men and the instrument of good. As a matter of fact, many of the most frequently and best translated *Odes* are devoid both of moral intent, and, in the ordinary sense, of moral effect. *To Pyrrha, Soracte Covered with*

*Snow, Carpe Diem, To Glycera, Integer Vitae,
To Chloe, Horace and Lydia, The Bandusian
Spring, Faunus, To an Old Wine-Jar, The End
of Love,* and *Beatus Ille* are merely *jeux-
d'esprit* of the sort that for the moment lighten
and clear the spirit. The same may be said
of *The Bore* and the *Journey to Brun-
disium* among the *Satires,* and of many of the
Epistles.

But these trifles light as air are nevertheless
of the sort for which mankind is eternally
grateful, because men are convinced, without
process of reason, that by them the fibre of life
is rested and refined and strengthened. We
may call this familiar effect by the less familiar
name of re-creative. What lover of Horace has
not felt his inmost being cleansed and refreshed
by the simple and exquisite art of *The Bandusian Spring,* whose cameo of sixty-eight Latin
words in four stanzas is an unapproachable
model of vividness, elegance, purity, and restraint:

O *crystal-bright Bandusian Spring,*
  Worthy thou of the mellow wine
And flowers I give to thy pure depths:
  A kid the morrow shall be thine.

[153]

The day of lustful strife draws on,
  The starting horn begins to gleam;
In vain! His red blood soon shall tinge
  The waters of thy clear, cold stream.

The dog-star's fiercely blazing hour
  Ne'er with its heat doth change thy pool;
To wandering flock and ploughworn steer
  Thou givest waters fresh and cool.

Thee, too, 'mong storied founts I'll place,
  Singing the oak that slants the steep,
Above the hollowed home of rock
  From which thy prattling streamlets leap.

Or who does not live more abundant life at
reading the *Chloe Ode*, with its breath of the
mountain air and its sense of the brooding
forest solitude, and its exquisite suggestion of
timid and charming girlhood?

"You shun me, Chloe, wild and shy
  As some stray fawn that seeks its mother
Through trackless woods. If spring-winds sigh,
  It vainly strives its fears to smother; —

"Its trembling knees assail each other
  When lizards stir the bramble dry; —
You shun me, Chloe, wild and shy
As some stray fawn that seeks its mother.

" And yet no Libyan lion I, —
No ravening thing to rend another;
Lay by your tears, your tremors by, —
A husband's better than a brother;
Nor shun me, Chloe, wild and shy
As some stray fawn that seeks its mother."

But there are those who demand of poetry
a usefulness more easily measurable than that
of recreation. In their opinion, it is improvement rather than pleasure which is the end of
art, or at least improvement as well as pleasure.
In this, indeed, the poet himself is inclined to
agree: " He who mingles the useful with the
pleasant by delighting and likewise improving
the reader, will get every vote."

Let us look for these more concrete results,
and see how Horace the person still lives in
the character of men, as well as Horace the
poet in the character of literature.

To appreciate this better, we must return to
the theme of Horace's personal quality. We
have already seen that in no other poet so fully
as in Horace is the reality of personal contact
to be felt. The lyrics, as well as the *Epistles*
and *Satires*, are almost without exception addressed to actual persons. So successful is this

attempt of the poet to speak from the page that it needs but the slightest touch of imagination to create the illusion that we ourselves are addressed. We feel, as if at first hand, all the qualities that went to make up Horace's character, — his good will, good faith, and good-nature, the depth and constancy of his friendship, his glow of admiration for the brave deed, the pure heart, and the steadfast purpose, his patient endurance of ill, his delight in men and things, his affection for what is simple and sincere, his charity for human weakness, his mildly ironical mood, as of one who is aware that he himself is not undeserving of the good-humored censure he passes on others, his clear vision of the sources of happiness, his reposeful acquiescence, and his elusive humor, which never bursts into laughter and yet is never far away from it. We are taken into his confidence, like old friends. He describes himself and his ways; he lets us share in his own vision of himself and in his amusement at the bustling and self-deluded world, and subtly conciliates us by making us feel ourselves partakers with him in the criticism of life. There is no better example in literature of personal magnetism.

And he is more than merely personal. He is sincere and unreserved. Were he otherwise, the delight of intimate acquaintance with him would be impossible. It is the real Horace whom we meet, — not a person on the literary stage, with buskins, pallium, and mask. Horace holds the mirror up to himself; rather, not to himself, but to nature in himself. Every side of his personality appears: the artist, and the man; the formalist, and the skeptic; the spectator, and the critic; the gentleman in society, and the son of the collector; the landlord of five hearths, and the poet at court; the stern moralist, and the occasional voluptuary; the vagabond, and the conventionalist. He is independent and unhampered in his expression. He has no exalted social position to maintain, and blushes neither for parentage nor companions. His philosophy is not School-made, and the fear of inconsistency never haunts him. His religion requires no subscription to dogma; he does not even take the trouble to define it. Politically, his duties have come to be also his desires. He will accept the favors of the Emperor and his ministers if they do not compromise his liberty or happiness. If they withdraw their gifts, he knows how to do without them, because he has already done without them. He conceals nothing, pretends to nothing, makes no excuses, suffers from no self-consciousness, exercises no reserve. There are few expressions of self in all literature so spontaneous and so complete. Horace has left us a portrait of his soul much more perfect than that of his person. It is a truthful portrait, with both shadow and light.

And there is a corollary to Horace's frankness that constitutes another element in the charm of his personality. His very unreserve is the proof of an open and kindly heart. To call him a satirist at all is to necessitate his own definition of satire, "smilingly to tell the truth." At least in his riper work, there is no trace of bitterness. He laughs with some purpose and to some purpose, but his laughter is not sardonic. Sane judgment and generous experience tell him that the foibles of mankind are his own as well as theirs, and are not to be changed by so slight a means as a railing tongue. He reflects that what in himself has produced no very disastrous results may without great danger be forgiven also in them.

It is this intimate and warming quality in Horace that prompts Hagedorn to call him

" my friend, my teacher, my companion," and
to take the poet with him on country walks
as if he were a living person:

Horaz, mein Freund, mein Lehrer, mein Begleiter,
Wir gehen aufs Land. Die Tage sind so heiter;

and Nietzsche to compare the atmosphere of the
Satires and *Epistles* to the " geniality of a warm
winter day "; and Wordsworth to be attracted
by his appreciation of "the value of compan-
ionable friendship "; and Andrew Lang to address to him the most personal of literary
letters; and Austin Dobson to give his Horatian poems the form of personal address; and
countless students and scholars and men out of
school and immersed in the cares of life to
carry Horace with them in leisure hours.
Circum praecordia ludit, " he plays about the
heartstrings," said Persius, long before any of
these, when the actual Horace was still fresh
in the memory of men.

If we were to take detailed account of certain qualities missed in Horace by the modern
reader, we should be even more deeply convinced of his power of personal attraction. He
is not a Christian poet, but a pagan. Faith in

immortality and Providence, penitence and penance, and humanitarian sentiment, are hardly to be found in his pages. He is sometimes too unrestrained in expression. The unsympathetic or unintelligent critic might charge him with being commonplace.

Yet these defects are more apparent than real, and have never been an obstacle to souls attracted by Horace. His pages are charged with sympathy for men. His lapses in taste are not numerous, and are, after all, less offensive than those of European letters today, after the coming of sin with the law. And he is not commonplace, but universal. His content is familiar matter of today as well as of his own time. His delightful natural settings are never novel, romantic, or forced; we have seen them all, in experience or in literature, again and again, and they make familiar and intimate appeal. Phidyle is neither ancient nor modern, Latin nor Teuton; she is all of them at once. The exquisite expressions of friendship in the odes to a Virgil, or a Septimius, are applicable to any age or nationality, or any person. The story of the town mouse and country mouse is always old and always new, and always true. *Mutato nomine de te* may be said of it, and of all Horace's other stories; alter the names, and the story is about you. Their application and appeal are universal.

"Without sustained inspiration, without profundity of thought, without impassioned song," writes Duff, "he yet pierces to the universal heart. . . . His secret lies in sanity rather than impetus. Kindly and shrewd observer of the manifold activities of life, he draws vignettes therefrom and passes judgments thereon which awaken undying interest. *Non omnis moriar* — he remains fresh because he is human."

Horace's philosophy of life may be imperfect for the militant humanitarian and the Christian, but, as a matter of fact, it is a complete and perfect thing in itself. Horace does not fret or fume. He is not morbid or unpleasantly melancholy. It is true that "his tempered and polished expression of common experience, free from transports and free from despairs, speaks more forcibly to ripe middle age than to youth," but it is not without its appeal also to youth. Horace sums up an attitude toward existence which all men, of whatever nation or time, can easily understand, and which all, at some moment or other, sympathize with.

Whether they believe in his philosophy of life or not, whether they put it into practice or not, it is always and everywhere attractive, — attractive because founded on clear and sympathetic vision of the joys and sorrows that are the common lot of men, attractive because of its frankness and manly courage, and, above all, attractive because of its object. So long as the one great object of human longing is peace of mind and heart, no philosophy which recognizes it will be without followers. The Christian is naturally unwilling to adopt the Horatian philosophy as a whole, but with its *summum bonum,* and with many of its recommendations, he is in perfect accord. Add Christian faith to it, or add it, so far as is consonant, to Christian faith, and either is enriched.

We are better able now to appreciate the dynamic power of Horace the person. We may see it at work in the fostering of friendly affection, in the deepening of love for favorite spots of earth, in the encouragement of righteous purpose, in the true judging of life's values.

Horace is the poet of friendship. With his address to " Virgil, the half of my soul," his references to Plotius, Varius, and Virgil as the

purest and whitest souls of earth, his affectionate messages in *Epistle* and *Ode,* he sets the
heart of the reader aglow with love for his
friends. "Nothing, while in my right mind,
would I compare to the delight of a friend!"
What numbers of men have had their hearts
stirred to deeper love by the matchless ode to
Septimius:

> "*Septimius, who with me would brave*
> *Far Gades, and Cantabrian land*
> *Untamed by Rome, and Moorish wave*
> *That whirls the sand;*

> "*Fair Tibur, town of Argive kings,*
> *There would I end my days serene,*
> *At rest from seas and travelings,*
> *And service seen.*

> "*Should angry Fate those wishes foil,*
> *Then let me seek Galesus, sweet*
> *To skin-clad sheep, and that rich soil,*
> *The Spartan's seat.*

> "*Oh, what can match the green recess,*
> *Whose honey not to Hybla yields,*
> *Whose olives vie with those that bless*
> *Venafrum's fields?*

[163]

" *Long springs, mild winters glad that spot*
  By Jove's good grace, and Aulon, dear
 To fruitful Bacchus, envies not
  Falernian cheer.

" *That spot, those happy heights desire*
  Our sojourn; there, when life shall end,
 Your tear shall dew my yet warm pyre,
  Your bard and friend."

And what numbers of men have taken to
their hearts from the same ode the famous

> Ille terrarum mihi praeter omnes
> Angulus ridet, —

> *Yonder little nook of earth*
> *Beyond all others smiles on me,* —

and expressed through its perfect phrase the
love they bear their own beloved nook of earth.
" Happy Horace! " writes Sainte-Beuve on the
margin of his edition, " what a fortune has
been his! Why, because he once expressed in
a few charming verses his fondness for the life
of the country and described his favorite corner
of earth, the lines composed for his own
pleasure and for the friend to whom he addressed them have laid hold on the memory of

[164]

all men and have become so firmly lodged there
that one can conceive no others, and finds only
those when he feels the need of praising his own
beloved retreat!"

To speak of sterner virtues, what a source
of inspiration to righteousness and constancy
men have found in the apt and undying phrases
of Horace! "Cornelius de Witt, when con-
fronting the murderous mob; Condorcet, per-
ishing in the straw of his filthy cell; Herrick,
at his far-away old British revels; Leo, during
his last days at the Vatican, and a thousand
others," strengthened their resolution by re-
peating *Iustum et tenacem:*

> " *The man of firm and noble soul*
>   *No factious clamors can control*
>   *No threat'ning tyrant's darkling brow*
>   *Can swerve him from his just intent. . . .*
> *Ay, and the red right arm of Jove,*
> *Hurtling his lightnings from above,*
> *With all his terrors then unfurl'd,*
>   *He would unmoved, unawed behold:*
> *The flames of an expiring world*
>   *Again in crashing chaos roll'd,*
> *In vast promiscuous ruin hurl'd,*
> *Must light his glorious funeral pile:*
> *Still dauntless midst the wreck of earth he'd smile."*

Of this passage Stemplinger records thirty-one imitations. How many have had their patriotism strengthened by *Dulce et decorum est pro patria mori,* the verse which is aptly found in modern Rome on the monument to those who fell at Dogali. How many have been supported and comforted in calamity and sorrow by the poet's immortal words of consolation on the death of Quintilius:

> Durum: sed levius fit patientia
>   Quicquid corrigere est nefas, —

> *Ah, hard it is! but patience lends*
> *Strength to endure what Heaven sends.*

The motto of Warren Hastings was *Mens aequa in arduis,* — An even temper in times of trial. Even humorous use of these phrases has served a purpose. The French minister, compelled to resign, no doubt drew substantial consolation from *Virtute me involvo,* when he turned it to fit his case:

> *In the robe of my virtue I wrap me round*
>   *A solace for loss of all I had;*
> *But ah! I realize I've found*
>   *What it really means to be lightly clad!*

[166]

But the most pronounced effect of Horace's dynamic power is its inspiration to sane and truthful living. Life seems a simple thing, yet there are many who miss the paths of happiness and wander in wretched discontent because they are not bred to distinguish between the false and the real. We have seen the lesson of Horace: that happiness is not from without, but from within; that it is not abundance that makes riches, but attitude; that the acceptation of worldly standards of getting and having means the life of the slave; that the fraction is better increased by division of the denominator than by multiplying the numerator; that unbought riches are better possessions than those the world displays as the prizes most worthy of striving for. No poet is so full of inspiration as Horace for those who have glimpsed these simple and easy yet little known secrets of living. Men of twenty centuries have been less dependent on the hard-won goods of this world because of him, and lived fuller and richer lives. Surely, to give our young people this attractive example of sane solution of the problem of happy living is to leaven the individual life and the life of the social mass.

IV. CONCLUSION

WE have visualized the person of Horace and made his acquaintance. We have seen in his character and in the character of his times the sources of his greatness as a poet. We have seen in him the interpreter of his own times and the interpreter of the human heart in all times. We have traced the course of his influence through the ages as both man and poet. We have seen in him not only the interpreter of life, but a dynamic power that makes for the love of men, for righteousness, and for happier living. We have seen in him an example of the word made flesh. "He has forged a link of union," writes Tyrrell, "between intellects so diverse as those of Dante, Montaigne, Bossuet, La Fontaine, Voltaire, Hooker, Chesterfield, Gibbon, Wordsworth, Thackeray."

To know Horace is to enter into a great communion of twenty centuries,— the communion of taste, the communion of charity, the communion of sane and kindly wisdom, the communion of the genuine, the communion of righteousness, the communion of urbanity and of friendly affection.

"Farewell, dear Horace; farewell, thou wise and kindly heathen; of mortals the most human, the friend of my friends and of so many generations of men."

NOTES AND BIBLIOGRAPHY

The following groups of references are not meant as
annotations in the usual sense. Those to the text of the
poet are for such persons as wish to increase their
acquaintance with Horace by reading at first hand the
principal poems which have inspired the essayist's conclusions. The others are for those who desire to view
in detail the working of the Horatian influence.

HORACE THE PERSON:
> *Odes*, I. 27; 38; II. 3; 7; III. 8; IV. 11.
> *Satires*, I. 6; 9; II. 6.
> *Epistles*, I. 7; 10; 20.
> Suetonius, *Life of Horace.* (see below.)

HORACE THE POET:
> *Odes*, I. 1; 3; 6; 12; 24; 35; II. 7; 16; III. 1; 21;
> 29; IV. 2; 3; 4.
> *Satires*, I. 4; 6.
> *Epistles*, I. 3; 20; II. 2.

HORACE THE INTERPRETER OF HIS TIMES:
> Landscape; *Odes*, I. 4; 31; II. 3; 6; 14; 15; III.
> > 1; 13; 18; 23.
> > *Epistles*, I. 12; 14.
> Living; *Odes*, I. 1; III. 1; 2; 4; 6; IV. 5; *Epode*, 2.
> > *Satires*, I. 1; II. 6.
> > *Epistles*, I. 7; 10.
> Religion; *Odes*, I. 4; 10; 21; 30; 31; 34; III. 3;
> > 13; 16; 18; 22; 23; IV. 5; 6; *Epode*, 2
> Popular Wisdom; *Epistle*, I. 1; 4; II. 2.

HORACE THE PHILOSOPHER OF LIFE:
> The Spectator and Essayist; *Satires*, I. 4; II. 1.

The Vanity of Human Wishes;
>   *Odes*, I. 4; 24; 28; II. 13; 14; 16; 18; III. 1;
>   16; 24; 29; IV. 7.
>   *Satires*, I. 4; 6.
Epistles, I. 1.
The Pleasures of this World;
>   *Odes*, I. 9; 11; 24; II. 3; 14; III. 8; 23; 29;
>   IV. 12.
>   *Epistles*, I. 4.
Life and Morality;
>   *Odes*, I. 5; 18; 19; 27; III. 6; 21; IV. 13.
>   *Epistles*, I. 2; II. 1.
Life and Purpose;
>   *Odes*, I. 12; II. 2; 15; III. 2; 3; IV. 9; *Epode*, 2.
>   *Satires*, I. 1.
>   *Epistles*, I. 1.
The Sources of Happiness;
>   *Odes*, I. 31; II. 2; 16; 18; III. 16; IV. 9.
>   *Satires*, I. 1; 6; II. 6.
>   *Epistles*, I. 1; 2; 6; 10; 11; 12; 14; 16.

HORACE THE PROPHET:
>   *Odes*, II. 20; III. 1; 4; 30; IV. 2; 3.

HORACE AND ANCIENT ROME:
>   *Odes*, IV. 3.
>   *Epistles*, I. 20.
>   Suetonius, *Vita Horati, Life of Horace*, Translation,
>   J. C. Rolfe, in *The Loeb Classical Library*, New
>   York, 1914.
>   Hertz, Martin, *Analecta ad carminum Horatianorum
>   Historiam*, i-v. Breslau, 1876–82.
>   Schanz, Martin, *Geschichte der Römischen Litteratur*.
>   München, 1911.

HORACE AND THE MIDDLE AGE:
>   Manitius, Maximilian, *Analekten zur Geschichte des
>   Horaz im Mittelalter, bis 1300*. Göttingen, 1893.

HORACE AND MODERN TIMES:

    In Italy; Curcio, Gaetano Gustavo, *Q. Orazio Flacco, studiato in Italia dal secolo XIII al XVIII.* Catania, 1913.

    In France and Germany; Imelmann, J., *Donec gratus eram tibi, Nachdichtungen und Nachklänge aus drei Jahrhunderten.* Berlin, 1899.

        Stemplinger, Eduard, *Das Fortleben der Horazischen Lyrik seit der Renaissance.* Leipzig, 1906.

    In Spain; Menéndez y Pelayo, D. Marcelino, *Horacio en España*, 2 vols. Madrid, 1885.[2]

    In England; Goad, Caroline, *Horace in the English Literature of the Eighteenth Century.* New Haven, 1918.

        Myers, Weldon T., *The Relations of Latin and English as Living Languages in England during the Age of Milton.* Dayton, Virginia, 1913.

        Nitchie, Elizabeth, "Horace and Thackeray," in *The Classical Journal*, XIII. 393–410 (1918).

        Shorey, Paul, and Laing, Gordon J., *Horace: Odes and Epodes* (Revised Edition). Boston, 1910.

        Thayer, Mary R., *The Influence of Horace on the Chief English Poets of the Nineteenth Century.* New Haven, 1916.

HORACE THE DYNAMIC:

    Ars Poetica.

    Cowl, R. P., *The Theory of Poetry in England; its development in doctrines and ideas from the sixteenth century to the nineteenth century.* London, 1914.

    Dobson, Henry Austin, *Collected Poems*, Vol. I, 135, 181, 219, 222, 224, 231, 236, 245, 263; II. 66, 83, 243, etc. London, 1899.

    Gladstone, W. E., *The Odes of Horace*, English Verse Translation. New York, 1901.

    Kipling, Rudyard, et Graves, C. L., *Q. Horati Flacci Carminum Liber Quintus.* New Haven, 1920.[3]

NOTES AND BIBLIOGRAPHY

Lang, Andrew, *Letters to Dead Authors.* New York, 1893.

Martin, Sir Theodore, *The Odes of Horace;* translated into English verse. London, 1861.[2]

Untermeyer, Louis, " — *and Other Poets."* New York, 1916.

Whicher, G. M. and G. F., *On the Tibur Road, a Freshman's Horace.* Princeton, 1912.

Besides the works mentioned above, reference should be made to:

CAMPAUX, A., *Des raisons de la popularité d'Horace en France.* Paris, 1895.

D'ALTON, J. F., *Horace and His Age.* London, 1917.

McCREA, N. G., *Horatian Criticism of Life.* New York, 1917.

STEMPLINGER, EDUARD, *Horaz im Urteil der Jahrhunderte.* Leipzig, 1921.

TAYLOR, HENRY OSBORN, *The Classical Heritage of the Middle Ages.* New York, 1903.[2]

The Century Horace.

and, also, to the two following works, cited and quoted in the text:

DUFF, J. WIGHT, *A Literary History of Rome.* London, 1910.[2] (p. 545)

TYRRELL, R. Y., *Latin Poetry.* Boston, (lectures delivered at The Johns Hopkins University, 1893). (p. 164)

Note: Translations of Horace, not otherwise assigned or not enclosed in quotation marks, are those of G. S.

Our Debt to Greece and Rome

AUTHORS AND TITLES

HOMER. *John A. Scott.*

SAPPHO. *David M. Robinson.*

EURIPIDES. *F. L. Lucas.*

ARISTOPHANES. *Louis E. Lord.*

DEMOSTHENES. *Charles D. Adams.*

THE POETICS OF ARISTOTLE. *Lane Cooper.*

GREEK RHETORIC AND LITERARY CRITICISM. *W. Rhys Roberts.*

LUCIAN. *Francis G. Allinson.*

CICERO AND HIS INFLUENCE. *John C. Rolfe.*

CATULLUS. *Karl P. Harrington.*

LUCRETIUS AND HIS INFLUENCE. *George Depue Hadzsits.*

OVID. *Edward Kennard Rand.*

HORACE. *Grant Showerman.*

VIRGIL. *John William Mackail.*

SENECA THE PHILOSOPHER. *Richard Mott Gummere.*

APULEIUS. *Elizabeth Hazelton Haight.*

MARTIAL. *Paul Nixon.*

PLATONISM. *Alfred Edward Taylor.*

ARISTOTELIANISM. *John L. Stocks.*

STOICISM. *Robert Mark Wenley.*

LANGUAGE AND PHILOLOGY. *Roland G. Kent.*

AUTHORS AND TITLES

Aeschylus and Sophocles. *J. T. Sheppard.*

Greek Religion. *Walter Woodburn Hyde.*

Survivals of Roman Religion. *Gordon J. Laing.*

Mythology. *Jane Ellen Harrison.*

Ancient Beliefs in The Immortality of The Soul. *Clifford H. Moore.*

Stage Antiquities. *James Turney Allen.*

Plautus and Terence. *Gilbert Norwood.*

Roman Politics. *Frank Frost Abbott.*

Psychology, Ancient and Modern. *G. S. Brett.*

Ancient and Modern Rome. *Rodolfo Lanciani.*

Warfare by Land and Sea. *Eugene S. McCartney.*

The Greek Fathers. *James Marshall Campbell.*

Greek Biology and Medicine. *Henry Osborn Taylor.*

Mathematics. *David Eugene Smith.*

Love of Nature among the Greeks and Romans. *H. R. Fairclough.*

Ancient Writing and its Influence. *B. L. Ullman.*

Greek Art. *Arthur Fairbanks.*

Architecture. *Alfred M. Brooks.*

Engineering. *Alexander P. Gest.*

Modern Traits in Old Greek Life. *Charles Burton Gulick.*

Roman Private Life. *Walton Brooks McDaniel.*

Greek and Roman Folklore. *William Reginald Halliday.*

Ancient Education. *J. F. Dobson.*